Proverbial Democracy

Wolfgang Mieder

Proverbial Democracy

Government of the People, by the People, for the People

PETER LANG
New York · Berlin · Bruxelles · Chennai · Lausanne · Oxford

Bibliographic information published by the Deutsche Nationalbibliothek
The German National Library lists this publication in the German National Bibliography; detailed bibliographic data is available on the Internet at http://dnb.d-nb.de.

Library of Congress Cataloging-in-Publication Data
A CIP catalog record for this book has been applied for at the Library of Congress.

ISBN 978-3-0343-6567-3 (Print)
ISBN 978-3-0343-6568-0 (ePDF)
ISBN 978-3-0343-6569-7 (ePUB)
DOI 10.3726/b23809

Published by Peter Lang Publishing Inc., New York, USA

info@peterlang.com

This publication has been peer reviewed.

www.peterlang.com

Contact for General Product Safety Regulation (GPSR): gpsr@peterlang.com

Contents

Preface

At the time of the semiquincentennial of the signing of the American Declaration of Independence on July 4, 1776, its famous preamble "We hold these truths to be self-evident, that all men are created equal, that they are endowed by their Creator with certain unalienable rights, that among these are life, liberty and the pursuit of happiness – that to secure these rights, governments are instituted among men, deriving their just powers from the consent of the governed" will be cited innumerable times. Hopefully it will also be remembered that the early feminist Elizabeth Cady Stanton amended this revolutionary statement to the more inclusive "that all men and women are created equal" at the beginning of her unforgettable speech of July 19, 1848 at Seneca Falls, New York. In any case, together or in two parts, "All men are created equal" and "Life, liberty, and the pursuit of happiness" have long become proverbial and belong to the basic principles of the American sociopolitical life. But the declaration goes on to insist that to secure these rights a government needs to be formed whose powers come from the people. By the middle of the nineteenth century a companion phrase became current that expresses perhaps the most concise and best definition of what the Founding Fathers had in mind for a democracy: "Government of the people, by the people, for the people." It has long become proverbial and is cited in speeches and writings as often as the earlier declarative statement.

What follows in these pages is a detailed survey of the origin, history, meaning, and use of the proverbial triad starting with rudimentary attempts of formulating it in 1794 by Thomas Cooper, followed by John Adams in 1798, John Marshall in 1819, and with Daniel Webster eventually having his go at it in a speech of 1830. The actual tripartite structure before Lincoln came into its own in several variants in the significant writings of the abolitionist Theodore Parker in the 1850s. He in turn influenced Abraham Lincoln in his well-known conclusion of the Gettysburg Address of November 19, 1863: "that this nation, under God, shall have a new birth of freedom – and that government of the people, by the people, for the people, shall not perish from the earth." There was a time when most American school children learned the entire address of merely 272 words by heart. But no matter, Lincoln's "Government of the people, by the people, for the people" has gained such general currency that it rightfully has become a well-known proverbial definition of democracy far beyond the United States.

It is the survival of the "people"-triad that is discussed in this small book by way of numerous contextualized references based on Lincoln's memorable words. In the nineteenth century Frederick Douglass and Elizabeth Cady Stanton helped to spread the good word, but the phrase also caught on in literary writings and in the press. In the first half of the twentieth century Theodore Roosevelt, Calvin Coolidge, and especially Franklin D. Roosevelt, Winston Churchill, and Harry S. Truman drew on this democratic principle in their speeches and essays. Presidents like Dwight D. Eisenhower, John F. Kennedy, Lyndon B. Johnson, Richard Milhaus Nixon, Gerald Ford, Jimmy Carter, Ronald Reagan, George Bush, and Bill Clinton all followed suit, always stressing that the ideal government is one that is of, by, and for the people. In more recent years Presidents George W. Bush, Barack Obama, Joe Biden, and Donald Trump have also made sure that the message of the democratic proverb stays alive, with important politicians like Hillary Rodham Clinton and Bernie Sanders relying on the wisdom of the triad as well. All of this is discussed in considerable length throughout these pages together with additional references from political and journalistic writings. The emerging insight from this extensive documentation is that "Government of the people, by the people, for the people" is indeed the best definition of a proverbial democracy!

If I may add a personal note: In 1960, at the age of 16, I came to the United States on my own as a youthful immigrant from Germany. In due time I became a University Distinguished Professor of German and Folklore at the University of Vermont, where I taught for 50 years and pursued my studies on fairy tales, legends, folksongs, and above all proverbs. Some of my books deal with the proverbial rhetoric of Abraham Lincoln, Frederick Douglass, Elizabeth Cady Stanton and Susan B. Anthony, Harry S. Truman, Franklin Delano Roosevelt, John F. Kennedy, Martin Luther King, Ronald Reagan, and Barack Obama, and it is with joy that I look back on my co-authored comprehensive *Dictionary of American Proverbs* (New York: Oxford University Press, 1992), a considerable accomplishment and honor for a German-American. As such, my studies on the nature and politics of American proverbs have meant the world to me, and it is with much excitement that I present this study about proverbial democracy with thankfulness for my scholarly life as a naturalized citizen of the United States.

Wolfgang Mieder
Spring 2026

Proverbial Democracy: "Government of, by, for the People"

Abraham Lincoln's closing remarks of his short yet famous Gettysburg Address of November 19, 1863, have become proverbial as "Government of the people, by the people, for the people." Yet, as is the case with some of his other famous utterances like "A house divided against itself cannot stand," "Right makes might," and "Don't swap horses in midstream," he relied on the wisdom and insights of others to create his memorable phrase that provides a most succinct definition of democracy. Already on May 9, 1901, Samuel A. Green made the following observation on the widespread distribution and currency of this American credo:

> One short clause at the very end of this speech has been quoted on various occasions so often that it is now as familiar as a household word. I refer to the expression: "That this nation, under God, shall have a new birth of freedom, and that government of the people, by the people, for the people, shall not perish from the earth." The sentiment here contained is so simple, and defines a democracy so clearly and tersely, that it seems somewhat singular that the same idea has never been fully expressed before; as the Preacher says: "There is no new thing under the sun."
>
> Samuel A. Green, *President Lincoln's Speech at Gettysburg, November 19, 1863* (Boston: Massachusetts Historical Society, 1901), p. 1 (the entire pamphlet comprises a mere three pages).

Green then proceeds to refer to somewhat similar statements by Thomas Cooper (1794), an address presented to President John Adams (1798), Chief

Justice John Marshall (1819), Daniel Webster (1830), Alphonse de Lamartine (1850), and Theodore Parker (1850), and there is, as expected, a whole series of subsequent attempts to find precursors to Lincoln's profound statement. It will be the task of this study to trace this history of the phrase in much more detail by citing references in context. But the story does not end there, since Lincoln's unique formulation turned from a quotable definition of democracy to a generally known democratic proverb. As such it has survived in numerous and very different contexts to this day, and this development needs to be told as well.

Lexicographical Accounts of the "People"-Triad

The British journal *Notes & Queries* included several short paragraphs between 1908 and 1916 on the phrase, drawing attention to earlier versions of the triad by John Marshall (1819), Daniel Webster (1830), Theodore Parker (1850 and 1854), and, of course, Abraham Lincoln as the last link in this chain (see *Notes & Queries*, 10th series, 9 (1908), 10; 12th series, 1 (1916), 127 and 197, and 12th series, 2 (1916), 14–15). More modern lexicographers followed suit in their various dictionaries of quotations. Of special importance is Kate Louise Roberts's completely revised and enlarged *Hoyt's New Cyclopedia of Practical Quotations* (New York: Funk and Wagnalls, 1922: 332–335) with references to Thomas Cooper (1794), John Adams (1798), John Marshall (1819), Benjamin Disraeli (1827), Daniel Webster (1830), Lamartine (1850), Theodore Parker (1850, 1854, and 1858), and Abraham Lincoln (1863). Of major significance is also the reliable *Home Book of Proverbs, Maxims, and Famous Phrases* (New York: Macmillan, 1948: 549) by Burton Stevenson, which adds the names of Lord John Russell (1831), J. R. Lowell (1884), Oscar Wilde (1895), and Michael Arlen (1939) to the list of references, thus actually taking the recorded history of the phrase beyond Lincoln for once. Subsequent compilers of quotation dictionaries do not equal the number of references of these two early standard works, to wit William Safire, *Political Dictionary* (New York: Random House, 1978: 319–320), John Bartlett, *Familiar Quotations* (Boston: Little, Brown and Company, 1992: 450), and Nigel Rees, *Cassell Companion to Quotations* (London: Cassell, 1997: 355–356). But Gregory Titelman ascribes a correct proverbial character to the well-known phrase in his *Dictionary of Popular Proverbs and Sayings* (New York: Random House, 1996: 124), and mentions Daniel Webster, Theodore Parker, and Abraham Lincoln, while at the same time also referring to the modern use of the phrase by Bel Kaufman (1964) and Walter Mondale (1984). Finally, Fred R. Shapiro registers Lincoln's statement with a reference to Daniel Webster's and Theodore Parker's earlier formulations in his magisterial *The New Yale Book of Quotations* (New Haven, Connecticut: Yale University Press, 2021: 493).

Clearly scholars tracing the history and dissemination of a particular expression must not only look for its possible sources but should also investigate how the particular quotation turned proverb lives on in various contexts. One thing is for certain, E. D. Hirsch and his co-authors were correct when they included the following statement in *The Dictionary of Cultural Literacy* (Boston: Houghton, Mifflin and Company, 1988: 244): "*government of the people, by the people, and for the people* Words from the GETTYSBURG ADDRESS of Abraham LINCOLN, often quoted as a definition of DEMOCRACY." Because of space constraints, this says very little, of course, and the same is true for the minimal contextual information given in the many dictionaries of phrases, proverbs, and quotations. More voluminous compilations might cite longer passages, but most often the references are unsatisfactory and at times simply copied from an earlier assemblage. What follows is an attempt to show a much more inclusive history of this proverbial definition of democracy, showing its somewhat different verbalization before Lincoln by John Marshall, Daniel Webster, Theodore Parker and others, then Lincoln's unique reformulation of it, and eventually its survival through a century and a half until the present day, noting especially the powerful employment of the statement by Frederick Douglass, Winston S. Churchill, Harry S. Truman, and many other political and literary figures as well as journalists and copy-writers of advertisements. The dictionaries already mentioned have provided a solid starting point for this study, but my own voluminous readings in American history, literature, and the mass media added many additional references. Also, the modern electronic search abilities yielded fascinating materials that would not have been located without the new world of databases. The result is a detailed chronological study of one of the most famous phrases of American history that expresses not only for this nation but for the entire world in a proverbial nutshell the underlying idea of a democracy.

Early Beginnings with John Adams and John Marshall

The earliest statement that has at least some resemblance with Abraham Lincoln's powerful triad is contained in an epistolary description of the new American government and society for a British friend that Thomas Cooper includes in his book entitled *Some Information Respecting America* (1794):

> You ask what appear to me to be the general inducements to people to quit England for America? In my mind, the first and principal feature is, *The total absence of anxiety respecting the future success of a family.* There is little fault to find with the government of America, either in principle or in practice: we have very few taxes to pay, and those are of acknowledged necessity, and moderate in amount: we have no animosities about religion; it is a subject about which no questions are asked: we have few respecting political men or political measures: the present irritation of men's minds in Great Britain, and the discordant state of society on political accounts, is not known there. The government is the government *of* the people, and *for* the people.
>
> Thomas Cooper, *Some Information Respecting America* (London: J. Johnson, 1794), pp. 52–53.

Even though Cooper uses but two elements of the triadic structure, he is already expressing the fundamental idea that a democratic government consists of the members of that society and exists for their benefit. Four years later, in early July of 1798, the citizens of the County of Westmoreland in Virginia sent a declaration of support to President John Adams which included this passage:

> The Declaration that our People are hostile to a Government made by themselves, for themselves and conducted by themselves is an Insult malignant in its Nature, and extensive in its Mischief. [...] That Freemen should differ in Opinion concerning the Measures of their Government is not only to be expected but is even to be desired when Obedient to Law and Guided by Love of Country. [...] Where is the Nation that can coerce United Columbia into Submission? The Sun has not yet shone upon it.
>
> *Proceedings of the American Antiquarian Society, at the Annual Meeting Held in Worcester, October 21, 1893* (Worcester, Massachusetts: Charles Hamilton, 1894), pp. 323–325.

Adams clearly was appreciative of this statement at a time when he was struggling with the possibility of having to go to war in Europe. On July

11, 1798, he took the time to respond to this supportive address by quoting the governmental triad from it, showing that he took an immediate liking to this definition of democracy about whose nature he had given so much thought in oral and written form:

> An address so replete with sentiments purely American and so respectful to me, subscribed with the Names of four hundred respectable Citizens of Virginia is to me of inestimable Value. The declaration that our People are hostile to a Government, made by themselves, for themselves, and conducted by themselves, if it were true, would be a demonstration that the people despise and hate themselves; this inference unnatural and shocking as it seems, is however, always literally true of a corrupted people.
>
> *Proceedings of the American Antiquarian Society, at the Annual Meeting Held in Worcester, October 21, 1893* (Worcester, Massachusetts: Charles Hamilton, 1894), pp. 326–327.

It should be noted, however, that Adams is merely quoting the Virginia declaration and that he did not originate this particular formulation. It also gained no currency in the public sphere but serves as an indication that the underlying idea of the phrase is in the air at this time.

Considerably closer to the proverbial triad is the following statement in William Wirt's early biography of Patrick Henry:

> The federalists who supported the measures of the new government, throughout, were accused by their adversaries of a disposition to strain the constructive powers of the constitution to their highest possible pitch; of a secret wish to convert the government into a substantial monarchy, at least. [...] They were branded with the name of *aristocrats*, a name of reproach borrowed from the parties in France; and were charged with being inimical to the cause of human liberty. [...] The party which urged [argued] these charges, took the name of republicans and democrats; declared themselves the friends of liberty and the people, and the firm advocates of a government of the people by the people.
>
> William Wirt, *Sketches of the Life and Character of Patrick Henry* (Philadelphia: James Webster, 1817), pp. 381–382.

Two years later there is yet another comment approaching the triad that Chief Justice John Marshall made in his "McCulloch v. Maryland" opinion of March 6, 1819: "The government of the Union, then, [...], is, emphatically and truly, a government of the people. In form and in substance it emanates from them. Its powers are granted by them, and are to be exercised directly on them, and for their benefit" (*The Papers of John Marshall*, ed. by Charles F. Hobson (Chapel Hill, North Carolina: University of North Carolina Press, 1995), vol. 8, p. 262). But this is not to say that some thoughts along these lines were not going on in Europe. The British statesman and novelist Benjamin Disraeli included these reflections on governmental power in his first novel *Vivian Grey* (1827), long before he became Prime Minister in the second half of the nineteenth century:

> We must not forget [...] that it is the business of those to whom Providence has allotted the responsible possession of power and influence — that it is their duty — [...] to become guardians of our weaker fellow-creatures — that all power is a trust — that we are accountable for its exercise — that, from the people, and for the people, all springs, and all must exist; and that, unless we conduct ourselves with the requisite wisdom, prudence, and propriety, the whole system of society will be disorganised; and this country, in particular, fall a victim to that system of corruption and misgovernment which has already occasioned the destruction of the great kingdoms mentioned in the Bible; and many other States besides — Greece, Rome, Carthage, etc.
>
> Benjamin Disraeli, *Vivian Grey* (London: Alexander Moring, 1904), vol. 2, p. 127.

Yet another masterful British statesman, Earl John Russell, followed suit on March 1, 1831, when he rose in Parliament in support of the Reform Bill (1832) for the House of Commons, once again showing that thoughts regarding the political future of the people were expressed in triads:

> To establish the Constitution on a firm basis, you must show that you are determined not to be the representatives of a small class, or of a particular interest; but to form a body [of government], who, representing the people, springing from the people, and sympathising with the people, can fairly call on the people to support the future burthens of the country, and to struggle with the future difficulties which it may have to encounter; confident that those who call upon them are ready to join them heart and hand: and are only looking, like themselves, to the glory and welfare of England.
>
> *Selections from Speeches of Earl Russell 1817 to 1841 and from Despatches 1859 to 1865* (London: Longmans, Green, and Co., 1870), pp. 335–336.

Sixteen years later, in France, Alphonse de Lamartine expressed similar views in his comprehensive study of the French Revolution with the title *Histoire des Girondins* (1847): "Ce but, c' était la souveraineté représentative de tous les citoyens. puisée dans une élection aussi large que le peuple lui-même, et agissant par le peuple et pour le peuple dans un conseill électif qui serait tout le gouvernement. L'ambition de Robespierre, si souvent calomniée alors et depuis, n'allait pas au-delà" (Alphonse de Lamartine, *Histoire des Girondins* (Paris: Plon, 1984), vol. 2, p. 445). An English translation of this analysis appeared in 1847, the year of its original publication: "This end was the representative sovereignty of all the citizens, concentrated in an election as extensive as the people themselves, and acting by the people, and for the people, in an elective council, which should be all the government. The ambition of Robespierre, so often calumniated then and since, went not beyond this" (Alphonse de Lamartine, *History of the Girondists*, translated by H. T. Ryde (London: Henry G. Bohn, 1864), vol. 3, p. 104). There might not have been much if any influence of the Disraeli or Lamartine formulations on the American scene, but they do show a definite preoccupation with the attempt to express in a succinct fashion the basic ideas of a democratic government.

Daniel Webster's Speech of January 26, 1830

There is no doubt that Abraham Lincoln was aware of Daniel Webster's definition and characterization of the American government which he included in a famous speech in the Senate of January 26, 1830, that dealt with the so-called Missouri Compromise of 1820, which admitted Missouri as a slave state and Maine as a free state while prohibiting slavery in territories that later became Kansas and Nebraska:

> It is the people's Constitution, the people's government, made for the people, made by the people, and answerable to the people. The people of the United States have declared that this Constitution shall be the supreme law. We must either admit the proposition, or dispute their authority. The States are, unquestionably, sovereign, so far as their sovereignty is not affected by this supreme law. But the State legislatures, as political bodies, however sovereign, are yet not sovereign over the people. [...] I hold it [the government] to be a popular government, erected by the people; those who administer it, responsible to the people; and itself capable of being amended and modified, just as the people

> may choose it should be. It is as popular, just as truly emanating from the people, as the State governments. [...] The people, then, erected this government. They gave it a Constitution, and in that Constitution they have enumerated the powers which they bestow on it. They have made it a limited government. They have defined its authority.
>
> *The Works of Daniel Webster* (Boston: Little, Brown and Company, 1853), vol. 3, pp. 321 and 333–334.

This is an extremely important argument for the singleness of the nation that is governed by laws that go beyond those of individual states. His argument for a national "people's government, made for the people, made by the people, and answerable to the people" is quite close to Lincoln's statement at the end of the Gettysburg Address some 30 years later, but it does not yet have the "proverbial ring" to it which Lincoln, the masterful rhetorical craftsman, was able to give to it.

This is also true for a similar description of the American form of government which Asher Robbins presents in his essay on "The American Revolution" (1841), namely "that the most powerful, the most prosperous, and the most happy of all governments, is the government of the people, by the people" (cited from Anne C. Lynch (ed.), *The Rhode-Island Book: Selections in Prose and Verse, from the Writings of Rhode-Island Citizens* (Providence, Rhode Island: H. Fuller, 1841), p. 160). This short binary formula of "government of the people, by the people" rings well in the ear, and it is slowly but surely becoming a rhetorical standard and will be picked up by Lincoln in due time. It is, however, not known and perhaps doubtful that he knew this particular essay, although he was an avid reader in such matters.

Major Importance of Theodore Parker's Speeches and Writings

In a speech of May 25, 1850, at a meeting of the citizens of Boston in Faneuil Hall, the clergyman, social reformer, and abolitionist Theodore Parker addressed the vexing problem that slavery presented to the nation, and his words mark the beginning of a constant flow of attempts by him to find the best wording for a short definition of the nature of the American government. In these early remarks, he has not yet found a concise triadic structure:

> It is a great question, comprising many smaller ones: – Shall we extend and foster Slavery, or shall we extend and foster Freedom? Slavery, with its consequences, material, political, intellectual, moral; or Freedom, with the consequences thereof? A question so important seldom comes to be decided before any generation of men. This age is full of great questions, but this of Freedom is the chief. It is the same question which in other forms comes up in Europe [revolutions of 1848]. This is presently to be decided here in the United States by the servants of the people, I mean, by the Congress of the nation; in the name of the people; for the people, if justly decided; against them, if unjustly. If it were to be left to-morrow to the naked votes of the majority, I should have no fear. But the public servants of the people may decide otherwise.
>
> Theodore Parker, *Speeches, Addresses, and Occasional Sermons* (Boston: Ticknor and Fields, 1861), vol. 3, p. 2.

But then, two months later on May 29, 1850, Parker found truly compelling words in his speech on "Slave Power in America" at a New England anti-slavery convention in Boston. Here he defines the American government in exactly the same way that Abraham Lincoln would do it 13 years later, but there is one considerable difference in that Parker adds the inclusive adjective "all" three times before the noun "people," clearly signaling that he means to include the hopefully soon to be freed slaves of the nation as well. His remarks belong to the most impressive statements of that period in American history, and they certainly deserve to stand next to those of Lincoln whose important utterances could obtain wider currency due to his leadership position:

> There is what I call the American idea. I so name it, because it seems to me to lie at the basis of all our truly original, distinctive and American institutions. It is itself a complex idea, composed of three subordinate and more simple ideas, namely: The idea that all men have unalienable rights; that in respect thereof, all men are created equal; and that government is to be established and sustained for the purpose of giving every man an opportunity for the enjoyment and development of all these unalienable rights. This idea demands, as the proximate organization thereof, a democracy , that is, a government of all the people, by all the people, for all the people; of course, a government after the principles of eternal justice, the unchanging law of God; for shortness' sake, I will call it the idea of Freedom.
>
> Theodore Parker, *Speeches, Addresses, and Occasional Sermons* (Boston: Ticknor and Fields, 1861), vol. 3, pp. 41–42.

This speech had its influence on Lincoln in many ways, notably on his repeated use of the statement that "all men are created equal; that they are endowed by their creator with certain unalienable rights; that among these are life, liberty, and the pursuit of happiness" from the Declaration of Independence (see Wolfgang Mieder, *The Proverbial Abraham Lincoln* (New York: Peter Lang, 2000), pp. 135–137 and 146–150), to which Parker is obviously alluding as well. Quite certainly Lincoln was influenced by Theodore Parker's use of the triadic structure of his government definition. When Lincoln concluded his Gettysburg Address on November 19, 1863, with the claim that the "government of the people, by the people, for the people, shall not perish from the earth," he gave it the concise and perfect form in which it survives. He can hardly be called the originator of this phrasal definition, but it was he who implanted it in the minds and worldview of his contemporaries and generations of Americans to come. Interestingly, Lincoln dropped out the inclusive word "all," and that is exactly where the historical, cultural, social, and political problem arises with Lincoln's proverb. Did he even include the African-American population in his thoughts when he spoke of a "government of the people, by the people, for the people?" After all, Lincoln's *Emancipation Proclamation* of January 1, 1863, had not yet brought suffrage to the former slaves, and women's right to vote was also not established yet. Thus the proverb appears as a privileged statement for white males, with Theodore Parker's more liberal statement proving the exception to the rule.

In any case, half a year later, Parker returned to his inclusive definition of a true democracy, but in his Thanksgiving sermon about "The State of the Nation" of November 28, 1850, he reduced his triad to an absolute minimum, dropping the noun "people" and using instead the nominalization of "all" to bring his point across that he does mean everybody:

> This democratic idea is founded in human nature, and comes from the nature of God who made human nature. To carry it out politically is to execute justice, which is the will of God. This idea, in its realization, leads to a democracy, a government of all, for all, by all. Such a government aims to give every man all his natural rights; it desires to have political power in all hands, property in all hands, wisdom in all heads, goodness in all hearts, religion in all souls.
>
> Theodore Parker, *Speeches, Addresses, and Occasional Sermons* (Boston: Ticknor and Fields, 1861), vol. 3, pp. 195–196.

It is hard to say whether Parker at this early date in American history thought of women in his claim that "every man" deserves the fair treatment of a democratic government, but be that as it may, he certainly includes the slaves as such. Linguistically it should be noted, however, that he has not yet found a repeatable formula for his triadic definition. Not only has he deleted the noun "people," he also changed the order of the prepositions of "of, by, for" (which Lincoln will use as well) to "of, for, by."

Be that as it may, Lincoln might also have known Parker's address "Some Thoughts on the Progress of America," which he delivered at an anti-slavery convention in Boston on May 31, 1854. Here Parker returned to his original triad with the same sequence of prepositions:

> First there is the Democratic Idea: that all men are endowed by their Creator with certain natural rights; that these rights are alienable only by the possessor thereof; that they are equal in all men; that government is to organize these natural, unalienable, and equal rights into institutions designed for the good of the governed; and therefore government is to be of all the people, by all the people, and for all the people. Here government is development, not exploitation.
>
> Theodore Parker, *Additional Speeches, Addresses, and Occasional Sermons* (Boston: Ticknor and Fields, 1861), vol. 2, p. 25.

Another four years later, on May 26, 1858, Parker delivered a speech at yet another New England anti-slavery convention on "The Relation of Slavery to a Republican Form of Government." This time he defines three forms of government, returning more or less to his truncated triad but changing the preposition "of" to the interesting variant "over":

> All society must have its government, that is, Rules of Conduct, and Conductors to see that they are kept. – Abstract Rules, Concrete Rulers. The substance of government consists in these two, and is always the same: but the forms thereof vary much from land to land, and age to age; yet may they be thus grossly summed in three:
>
> I. Monarchy – The One-Man Power; government over all, but by one, and often in practice it turns out to be chiefly for the sake of that one.
>
> II. Oligarchy – The Few-Men Power; government over all, but by a few, and often in practice it turns out to be chiefly for the sake of that few.

> III. Democracy – The All-Men Power; government over all, by all, and for the sake of all. Yet, practically, it must be government by the Majority, and in fact, it often turns out to be chiefly for the advantage of that majority. As a general rule, no majority, no small body of men, no individual man, is ever trusted with unlimited power over others, but he abuses it – for his gain, to their loss. Such is the friction in all social machinery.
>
> Theodore Parker, *The Relation of Slavery to a Republican Form of Government. A Speech Delivered at the New England Anti-Slavery Convention, Wednesday Morning, May 26, 1858* (Boston: William L Kent, 1858), pp. 4–5.

A little more than a month later, in his last great anti-slavery address on July 4, 1858, entitled "The Effect of Slavery on the American People," Parker uttered the following words in the Music Hall at Boston:

> Theocracy, the priest power; monarchy, the one-man power; and oligarchy, the few-men power – are three forms of vicarious government over the people, perhaps for them, not by them. Democracy is direct self-government, over all the people, by all the people, for all the people. Our institutions are democratic: theocratic, monarchic, oligarchic vicariousness is all gone.
>
> Theodore Parker, "The Effect of Slavery on the American People," in *The Collected Works of Theodore Parker*, ed. by Frances Power Cobbe (London: Trübner, 1863–1871), vol. 8, p. 138.

We know for a fact that Abraham Lincoln was aware of Parker's work at that time. His friend and early biographer William H. Herndon reports that he brought with him "additional sermons and lectures by Theodore Parker, who was warm in his commendation of Lincoln. One of these lectures was a lecture on 'The Effect of Slavery on the American People,' which was delivered in the Music Hall in Boston, and which I gave to Lincoln, who read and returned it. He liked especially the following expression, which he marked with a pencil, and which he in substance afterwards used in his Gettysburg address: 'Democracy is direct self-government, over all the people, for all the people, by all the people'" (William H. Herndon and Jesse W. Weik, *Abraham Lincoln. The True Story of a Great Life* (New York: D. Appleton, 1892), vol. 2, p. 65; see also John White Chadwick, *Theodore Parker. Preacher and Reformer* (Boston: Houghton, Mifflin and Company, 1900), p. 323).

There is one more reference from the influential writings and opinions by Theodore Parker that deserves to be cited here in conclusion. In his significant essay on "Transcendentalism" (published posthumously in 1876), Parker shows how much the ideal of a democratic government is not based on experience and precedents alone but that it starts from a consciousness of human nature, appealing to a natural justice and a harmonious and progressive development:

> The great political idea of America, the idea of the Declaration of Independence, is a composite idea made up of three simple ones: 1. Each man is endowed with certain unalienable rights. 2. In respect of these rights all men are equal. 3. A government is to protect each man in the entire and actual employment of all the unalienable rights. Now the first two ideas represent ontological facts, facts of human consciousness; they are facts of necessity. The third is an idea derived from the two others, is a synthetic judgment *a priori*; it was not learned from sensational experience; there never was a government which did this, nor is there now. Each of the other ideas transcended history: every unalienable right has been alienated, still is; no two men have been actually equal in actual rights. Yet the idea is true, capable of proof by human nature, not of verification by experience; as true as the proposition that three angles of a triangle are equal to two right angles; but no more capable of a sensational proof than that. The American Revolution, with American history since, is an attempt to prove by experience this transcendental proposition, to organize the transcendental idea of politics. The idea demands for its organization, a democracy — a government of all, for all, and by all; a government by natural justice, by legislation that is divine as much as true astronomy is divine, legislation which enacts law representing a fact of the universe, a resolution of God.
>
> Cited from Robert E. Collins, *Theodore Parker: American Transcendentalist. A Critical Essay and a Collection of His Writings* (Metuchen, New Jersey: The Scarecrow Press, 1973), pp. 49–74 (here pp. 66–67). It was published as *Transcendentalism. A Lecture.* Never before printed (Boston: Free Religious Association, 1876).

Not meaning to take anything away from Parker's philosophical and religious thoughts, he simply can't get his triple formula straight! This time it is "a government of all, for all, and by all," and this new variant is proof that the formula as such has not been solidified into a proverbial quotation by Parker himself let alone the general American population. It took Abraham Lincoln in his public role as President of the United States to accomplish this feat. But never could it be denied that Theodore Parker had a major influence on the political and social thought of Lincoln, including the definitive formulation of "government of the people, by the people, for the people" in his Gettysburg Address of 1863.

Abraham Lincoln as Catalyst and Phrase-Forger

Before turning to Lincoln's Gettysburg Address, it might do well to cite one more paragraph that includes the spirit albeit not the precise linguistic form of the triadic phrase. In 1857, W. Alfred Jones reflected on the American government in his essay on "Titles," chastising his fellow citizens for placing too much value on pomp and circumstance in the form of honors, ceremonies, titles, etc. This ought not to be so in a true democracy which he defines as follows:

> Democracy is a principle (political, not social), and does not depend upon the dress or pursuits or accomplishments of the individual professing it. It is a philanthropic and philosophic system of polity, wholly irrespective of personal habits or prejudices. It is the government of the people by themselves. Of this great body, the leaders (for the mass cannot act as one man, and must delegate duties and assign powers) are expected to be in advance, socially and intellectually, if not also morally and politically of their fellows, else why leaders? And we find as a matter of history, the staunchest advocates of liberal views and free government at all times, and especially in the most excited times, to have been able men, good patriots and gentlemen – to look at Lafayette in France; Sidney and Russell and Hampden in England; and all of our own great Revolutionary characters without exception.
>
> W. Alfred Jones, *Characters and Criticisms* (New York: I. Y. Westervelt, 1857), p. 239.

Admittedly, the phrasal segment "government of the people by themselves" is perhaps a mere allusion to the actual tripartite formula that is gaining in currency in the mid-1850s. But Lincoln had the same problem in his "Message to Congress in Special Session" of July 4, 1861, where he is justifying his decision to go to war with the rebelling Southern states:

> And this issue [the beginning of open hostilities and the possible break-up of the country over slavery] embraces more than the fate of these United States. It presents to the whole family of man, the question, whether a constitutional republic, or a democracy – a government of the people, by the same people – can, or cannot, maintain its territorial integrity, against its own domestic foes.

> It presents the question, whether discontented individuals, too few in numbers to control administration, according to organic law, in any case, can always, upon the pretences made in this case, or on any other pretences, or arbitrarily, without any pretence, break up their Government, and thus practically put an end to free government upon the earth. It forces us to ask: "Is there, in all republics, this inherent, and fatal weakness?" "Must a government, of necessity, be too *strong* for the liberties of its own people, or too *weak* to maintain its own existence?" So viewing the issue, no choice was left but to call out the war power of the Government; and so to resist force, employed for its destruction, by force, for its preservation.
>
> *The Collected Works of Abraham Lincoln*, ed. by Roy P. Basler (New Brunswick, New Jersey: Rutgers University Press, 1953), vol. 4, p. 426.

It is a bit surprising that Lincoln only used the bipartite phrase of "government of the people, by the same people" in this extremely important speech at the outset of the Civil War. Obviously the reading of speeches and essays by Webster and Parker had not ingrained the triadic phrase to such a degree that it flowed as a prefabricated formula into his political rhetoric at this time.

Since not even Webster or Parker had this precise influence on Lincoln, it is very doubtful indeed that the remarks which Louis Kossuth (1802–1894), the Governor of Revolutionary Hungary in 1849, made on February 7, 1852, before the Ohio Legislature at Columbus during a fund-raising trip to the United States, had any direct link to Lincoln's Gettysburg Address. At that time Kossuth observed that "The spirit of our age is Democracy. All for the people, and all by the people. Nothing *about* the people *without* the people. That is Democracy, and that is the ruling tendency of the spirit of our age" (cited from an article on "Ohio Legislature" in the *Ohio State Journal* (February 7, 1852), no pp.). The somewhat patriotic argument by Steven Béla Várdy in an article on "Louis Kossuth's Words in Abraham Lincoln's Gettysburg Address" (1999) goes too far in its claim that Kossuth's speech "was more than likely the source of inspiration for Abraham Lincoln's oft-recited masterpiece, the 'Gettysburg Address'." His arguments become even more questionable when one considers the errors in the concluding paragraph of the article:

> There is no doubt that Kossuth's and Lincoln's phrases *by the people, for the people*, are philologically identical. The question, however, remains whether the

> American President in 1864 knowingly and deliberately quoted the Kossuthian phrase or only accidently used the same words as Kossuth. If the identical phrasing is accidental, we can suppose that "by the people for the people" may have been a stereotype of American liberal journalism of the 50s and 60s in the last century. A comprehensive data collection on the phrase from the contemporary media could help to answer this puzzling question.
>
> Steven Béla Várdy, "Louis Kossuth's Words in Abraham Lincoln's Gettysburg Address," *Eurasian Studies Yearbook*, 71 (1999), 27–32 (here pp. 31–32).

First of all, the phrases by Kossuth and Lincoln are *not* philologically identical: Kossuth in 1852 has "all for the people, and all by the people," while Lincoln in 1863 (not 1864!) says "of the people, by the people, for the people." And who is to say that Lincoln came across the Kossuth speech in the *Ohio State Journal* of February 7, 1852? This is all but conjecture, and Várdy appears to be not at all aware of any of the references mentioned thus far in this study. He is, however, correct, that a comprehensive collection of data on the phrase will shed light on all of this, as the numerous references of this present survey illustrate.

There is no doubt that Lincoln "conned the texts of speeches made by Webster" (Earl W. Wiley, "Lincoln the Speaker 1816–1830," in Lionel Crocker (ed.), *An Analysis of Lincoln and Douglas as Public Speakers and Debaters* (Springfield, Illinois: Charles C. Thomas, 1968), p. 19), Parker, and others, and it is only natural that such careful studies led to rhetorical borrowings ranging from direct quotations to paraphrases and indirect allusions. As Lincoln prepared his numerous speeches, he would gather material from many sources and spend days "reading, listening, rephrasing, refocusing, and strengthening his arguments" (Waldo W. Braden, "'A Remorseless Analyzer': Lincoln's Speech Preparation," in Waldo W. Braden, *Lincoln: Public Speaker* (Baton Rouge, Louisiana: Louisiana State University Press, 1988), p. 51). Clearly no person works in absolute isolation, and as Byron D. Murray aptly and not at all defensively has pointed out, "it detracts nothing from Lincoln to say that he appears not to have written always out of the loneliness of his own mind, but to have reflected upon and given his own savour to some of the best expression of his time" (Byron D. Murray, "Lincoln Speaks," *Contemporary Review*, 208 (1966), 261). To suggest even the thought of plagiarism is utterly absurd, and the interrogatively phrased title of the journalistic essay "Lincoln: Rhetorical Copycat?" (1967) not only misses the point but suggests a *modus operandi* on the part of

Lincoln which does not hold water. One might, however, be inclined to agree with its author Thoburn V. Barker that in certain instances, including some of his famed utterances, "what he [Lincoln] said was customary rather than original, universal rather than unique" (Thoburn V. Barker, "Lincoln: Rhetorical Copycat?" *Today's Speech*, 15 (1967), 30 (the entire note on pp. 29–30). But it was he, Lincoln, who said what he said, when he said it, and how he said it. That cannot possibly be argued away or diminished in any way.

These considerations lead quite naturally to one of the most famous phrases attributed to Lincoln, namely the one included in the closing remarks of his short yet famous Gettysburg Address of November 19, 1863:

> Four score and seven years ago our fathers brought forth on this continent, a new nation, conceived in Liberty, and dedicated to the proposition that all men are created equal.
>
> Now we are engaged in a great civil war, testing whether that nation, or any nation so conceived and so dedicated, can long endure. We are met on a great battle-field of that war. We have come to dedicate a portion of that field, as a final meeting place for those who here gave their lives that that nation might live. It is altogether fitting and proper that we should do this.
>
> But in a larger sense, we can not dedicate – we can not consecrate – we can not hallow – this ground. The brave men, living and dead, who struggled here, have consecrated it, far above our poor power to add or detract. The world will little note, nor long remember what we say here, but it can never forget what they did here. It is for us the living, rather, to be dedicated here to the unfinished work which they who fought here have thus far so nobly advanced. It is rather for us to be here dedicated to the great task remaining before us – that from these honored dead we take increased devotion to that cause for which they gave their last full measure of devotion – that we here highly resolve that these dead shall not have died in vain – that this nation, under God, shall have a new birth of freedom - and that government of the people, by the people, for the people, shall not perish from the earth.
>
> *The Collected Works of Abraham Lincoln*, ed. by Roy P. Basler (New Brunswick, New Jersey: Rutgers University Press, 1953), vol. 7, pp. 18–23 (with variants); see also Garry Wills, *Lincoln at Gettysburg: The Words that Remade America* (New York: Touchstone, 1992), pp. 35–37.

When Lincoln added at the very end that a democratic government "shall not perish from the earth," he might well have had a passage from the Bible in mind: "Where there is no vision, the people perish: but he that keepeth the law, happy is he" (Proverbs 29:18). But regarding the precise wording of "government of the people, by the people, for the people," the phrase is indeed Lincoln's! Bi- and tripartite variants of it were in considerable oral and written circulation. But if there was any direct influence, it most likely was by Daniel Webster or even more obviously by Theodore Parker. Except for the word "all," Parker's phrase is absolutely identical with that of Lincoln, and the latter can hardly be considered the originator of this triadic formulation. That does not mean, of course, that Lincoln did not popularize his own version that excludes the "all" reference through his masterful Gettysburg Address so that it now has become a proverbial definition of a free and democratic government. In the precise wording of "Government of the people, by the people, for the people" with the occasional addition of "and" in later references, this statement turned memorable quotation and eventually having become a well-known proverb belongs to Abraham Lincoln – no doubt about it.

Frederick Douglass and His Repetitive Use of the Proverb

In all of his work for the steady improvement of the Black population, Lincoln's contemporary and friend, the former slave and subsequent abolitionist and sociopolitical reformer Frederick Douglass, never lost sight of his goal to fight for civil rights of all the people. In a bitter speech on January 17, 1850, in Syracuse, New York, he made this point very clearly, but this time still primarily from the point of view of the abolitionist: "Talk to me of the love of liberty of your Washingtons, Jeffersons, Henrys. They were strangers to any just idea of Liberty! He who does not love Justice and Liberty for all, does not love Liberty and Justice. They wrote of Liberty in the Declaration of Independence with one hand, and with the other clutched their brother by the throat! These are the men who formed the union! I cannot enter into it. Give me NO UNION WITH SLAVEHOLDERS!" (*The Frederick Douglass Papers*, ed. by John Blassingame (New Haven, Connecticut: Yale University Press, 1985–1992), vol. 2, p. 223). About six years later, on May 28, 1856, by chance in the same city of Syracuse, his message sounded much more inclusive: "It [the Constitution] does not know anything of Irishmen, Englishmen, or Germans, of white men or black men; but of *men*. It knows nothing of a north, south, east or west; but *the people*" (*The Frederick Douglass Papers*, vol. 3, p. 140). And another year later, on May 11, 1857, in New York, he speaks of "the people" and the Constitution by directly alluding to its preamble: "'We, the people' – not we, the white people – not we, the citizens, or the legal voters – not we, the privileged class, and excluding all other classes but we, the people; not we, the horses and cattle, but we the people – the men and women, the human inhabitants of the United States, do ordain and establish this Constitution, etc." (*The Frederick Douglass Papers*, vol. 3, p. 176). Douglass obviously delighted in this explication of the preamble of the Constitution, as can be seen from this somewhat expanded paragraph from his speech on "The Constitution of the United States: Is It Pro-Slavery or Anti-Slavery?" that he gave on March 26, 1860, at Glasgow, Scotland:

> But it has been said that negroes are not included in the benefits sought under the declaration of purposes. Whatever slaveholders may say, I think it comes with ill grace from abolitionists to say the negroes in America are not included in this declaration of purposes. The negroes are not included! Who says this? The constitution does not say they are not included, and how dare any other person, speaking for the constitution, say so? The constitution says "We the people;" the language is "we the people;" not we the white people, not we the citizens, not we the privileged class, not we the high, not we the low, not we of English extraction, not we of French or of Scotch extraction, but "we the people;" not we the horses, sheep, and swine, and wheelbarrows, but we the human inhabitants; and unless you deny that negroes are people, they are included within the purposes of this government. They are there, and if we the people are included, negroes are included; they have a right, in the name of the constitution of the United States, to demand their liberty.
>
> *The Frederick Douglass Papers*, vol. 3, p. 361.

It is always the integrity of the people that Douglass champions. When it comes to governing this nation, then all the people must count: "The beauty and perfection of government in our eyes will be attained when all the people under it, men and women, black and white, shall be conceded the right of equal participation in wielding its power and enjoying its benefits. Equality is even a more important word with us than liberty" (Aug. 24, 1871; cited from *The Life and Writings of Frederick Douglass*, ed. by Philip S. Foner (New York: International Publishers, 1950–1975), vol. 4, pp. 271–272). In his essay on "The Work of the Future" that appeared in November 1862 in *Douglass'*

Monthly, he put all of this quite succinctly into the formulaic statement: "The Government is not enthroned above the people but is of, by and through the people" (*The Life and Writings of Frederick Douglass*, vol. 3, p. 291). This almost proverbial statement precedes Lincoln's quite similar conclusion "government of the people, by the people, for the people" of the Gettysburg Address (November 19, 1863) by about a year. But once Douglass learned of Lincoln's formulation in the Gettysburg Address, he too started using it in that precise wording in numerous speeches, thus in fact adding to its popularity which resulted in its eventual proverbial status (Mieder 2001:88–94). In his major speech on the "Sources of Danger to the Republic," delivered on February 7, 1867, in St. Louis, he used it for the first time, starting the paragraph with a bit of folk humor by including the proverbial expression "dyed in the wool" to refer to himself as a true democrat, and not as a member of the Democratic but rather the Republican Party:

> In fact, I am here to-night as a democrat, a genuine democrat dyed in the wool. I am here to advocate a genuine democratic republic; to make this a republican form of government, purely a republic, a genuine republic; free it from everything that looks toward monarchy; eliminate all foreign elements, all alien elements from it; blot out from it everything antagonistic of republicanism declared by the fathers – that idea was that all governments derived their first powers from the consent of the governed; make it a government of the people, by the people and for the people, and for all the people, each for all and all for each; blot out all discrimination against any person, theoretically or practically, and make it conform to the great truths laid down by the fathers; keep no man from the ballot box or jury box or the cartridge box, because of his color – exclude no woman from the ballot box because of her sex. Let the government of the country rest securely down upon the shoulders of the whole nation; let there be no shoulder that does not bear up its proportion of the burdens of the government. Let there [be] no conscience, no intellect in the land not directly responsible for the moral character of the government – for the honor of the government. Let it be a genuine Republic, in which every man subject to it is represented in it, and I see no reason why a Republic may not stand while the world stands.
>
> *The Frederick Douglass Papers*, vol. 4, p. 158.

What a statement barely two years after the Civil War! What a vision for a positive Reconstruction of the nation "for all the people, each for all and all for each," without any discrimination by race or gender! He is clearly years ahead of major constitutional amendments in this ideal view of a new republic.

It must never be forgotten that "next to Abolition and the battle for equal rights for the Negro people, the cause closest to Douglass' heart was woman's rights" (*The Life and Writings of Frederick Douglass*, vol. 2, p. 15). Looking back on his life's work, Douglass stated with much linguistic insight: "In the old days, of slavery I began all my speeches with the saying, 'Every man is himself.' He lives and dies and is responsible for himself. What is true of man is true of woman. I affirm the individuality and self-ownership of women" (Dec. 3, 1884; *The Frederick Douglass Papers*, vol. 5, p. 169). In its more explicit contextualization, Douglass's use of Lincoln's famous phrase-turned-proverb goes further than what Lincoln had said in his Gettysburg Address. So why should Douglass's statement not stand next to Lincoln's and bear witness to the life of a man equal in stature to this great president? Pray that one of the next presidents of this nation might include this powerful statement in his or her inaugural address to give credit to a great champion of civil rights.

Fifteen years later, in an address on May 30, 1882, in Rochester, New York, Douglass incorporated the proverb into a global vision, indicating that he went far beyond the purely American interpretation of its wisdom. The breadth and depth of Douglass's thoughts on race, gender, and politics are indeed astounding in such statements that are as fitting today as they were in the nineteenth century:

> If the existence of society is more than the lives of individual men; if all history proves that no great addition has ever been made to the liberties of mankind, except through war; if progress of the human race has been disputed by force and it has only succeeded by opposing force with force; if nations are most effectively taught righteousness by affliction and suffering; if the eternal laws of rectitude are essential to the preservation, happiness and perfection of the human race; if there is anything in the world worth living for, fighting for and dying for, the suppression of our rebellion by force was not only a thing right and proper in itself but an immense and immeasurable gain to our country and the world. Had that rebellion succeeded with all its malign purposes, what then would have become of our grand example of free institutions, of what value then would have been our government of the people by the people and for the people? What ray of light would have been left above the horizon, to kindle the first hope for the toiling millions in Europe? Every despot in the Old World would have seen in our manifest instability of government, a new and powerful argument in favor of despotic power.
>
> *The Frederick Douglass Papers*, vol. 5, p. 48.

While Douglass has the entire "human race" of the "world" in mind, he obviously knew his American political and social history and its famous documents the best. This becomes evident in yet another speech on September 24, 1883, in Louisville, Kentucky, in which he blends segments of the Declaration of Independence with the Gettysburg Address, to stress once again his deep-rooted belief in equality of all people, in a concise oratorical masterpiece: "We hold it to be self-evident that no class or color should be the exclusive rulers of this country. If there is such a ruling class, there must of course be a subject class, and when this condition is once established this Government of the people, by the people and for the people, will have perished from the earth" (*The Frederick Douglass Papers*, vol. 5, p. 110). Two and a half years later, on April 16, 1886, in the nation's capital, Douglass uses the proverb once again with specific reference to Abraham Lincoln: "We may affirm what must be admitted by all, that under this form of government so happily described, and so faithfully upheld by the great and lamented Abraham Lincoln, as 'government of the people, by the people, and for the people,' this nation has become rich, great, progressive and strong" (*The Frederick Douglass Papers*, vol. 5, p. 218). How happy indeed would Lincoln have been had he lived to hear the leading spokesman of African Americans make this pronouncement.

Yet exactly two years later, on April 16, 1888, Douglass uses the same democratic proverb to illustrate that Reconstruction is not going all so well:

> Let us see what are the relations subsisting between the negro and the state and national governments. What support, what assistance he has received from either of them. Take his relation to the national government and we shall find him a deserted, a defrauded, a swindled, and an outcast man. In law, free; in fact, a slave. In law, a citizen; in fact, an alien; in law, a voter; in fact, a disfranchised man. In law his color is no crime; in fact, his color exposes him to be treated as a criminal. Toward him every attribute of a just government is contradicted. For him, it is not a government of the people, by the people, and for the people. Toward him, it abandons the beneficent character of a government, and all that gives a government the right to exist.
>
> *The Frederick Douglass Papers*, vol. 5, p. 369.

All of these citations show that Douglass's work as agitator and reformer was never done, and he dedicated much of his energy in his later life to the cause of women's suffrage. Once again Lincoln's proverb served him extremely well to agitate for this basic right: "And now I ask, What right have I, what right have you, what right has anybody who believes in a government of the people, by the people, and for the people, to deny to woman this full and complete citizenship? What right have I, what right have you, what right has anybody, thus to humiliate one-half of the human family? There is no such right outside of the right of the robber and the usurper!" (Sept. 22, 1887; *The Frederick Douglass Papers*, vol. 5, p. 262). Seven years later on January 9, 1894, Douglass picked up his proverbial *leitmotif* again in front of an audience in Washington, D.C., arguing vehemently against restricting the right of "uneducated" blacks to vote and for women's suffrage: "I cannot follow these gentlemen in their proposition to limit suffrage to the educated alone. I would not make suffrage more exclusive, but more inclusive. I would not have it embrace merely the elite, but would include the lowly. I would not only include the men, I would gladly include the women, and make our government in reality as in name a government of the people and of the whole people" (*The Frederick Douglass Papers*, vol. 5, p. 594). As is generally known, the nineteenth amendment giving women the right to vote was not passed until 1920, but Douglass deserves much credit for having supported women of all races in the struggle for universal suffrage.

It is well known that Lincoln and Douglass had their differences, but there was deep mutual respect and admiration that grew in Douglass, as he reflected and spoke on Lincoln on various occasions after the assassination. Both great men had many obstacles to overcome on their paths to become servants of others. Slavery and poverty characterize their respective youths, but then came that drive toward self-education by all means. To this were added hard work and fundamental moral principles that made "self-made men" *par excellence* out of them. Little wonder then that their ideals and dreams became joint in the extended proverb "Government of the people, by the people, and for the people, and for all the people!"

Beyond Lincoln and Douglass: Last Third of the Nineteenth Century

Despite Douglass's repeated use of the phrase, even he got the order of the prepositions wrong once in his revised biography *Life and Times of Frederick*

Douglass (1893). As a resident of greater Washington D.C., he certainly was well aware of its peculiar political situation:

> The District of Columbia is the one spot where there is no government for the people, of the people, and by the people. Its citizens submit to rulers whom they have had no choice in selecting. They obey laws which they had no voice in making. They have a plenty of taxation, but no representation. In the great questions of politics in the country they can march with neither army, but are relegated to the position of neuters.
>
> Frederick Douglass, *Autobiographies: Narrative of the Life of Frederick Douglass* [1845], *My Bondage and My Freedom* [1855], *Life and Times of Frederick Douglass* [1893] (New York: Library of America, 1994), p. 960.

Perhaps Douglass altered the structure of the triad on purpose, but be that as it may, the following definition of a "popular government" that John Cordner attempted on December 22, 1864, shows that he might not have had Lincoln's passage in his repertoire of ready-made phrases as yet: "Popular government, I define as a government of the people, by the people. Now this is what we have in Canada. With us, however, it is administered under the form of limited monarchy. But the difference here, as compared with the government of the United States, is formal, rather than substantial" (John Cordner, *The American Conflict: An Address, Spoken Before the New England Society of Montreal on 22 December, 1864* (Montreal: John Lovell, 1865), p. 30). But by the 1870s, the triad from Lincoln's Gettysburg Address appears well established among writers, as the following contextualized references show. In indirect reverence to Lincoln, authors often place the well-known phrase into quotation marks, or they mention Lincoln directly:

> 1872: No American can look over the history of this country without being devoutly thankful for the blessings of that freedom and unrestrained liberty which is ours, or fail to experience a growth in that noblest form of patriotism which declares that this Government of the people, by the people and for the people, *shall be maintained*!
>
> W. E. Hathaway, "A Sketch of Russian History," *The Ladies' Repository*, 9, issue 6 (June 1872), pp. 408–409.
>
> 1874: So far as churches are concerned, they undeniably promote that public intelligence, conscientiousness, and moral purity, without which society would

utterly perish in its own corruption, and democratic government "of the people, by the people, for the people," would be impossible.

Lyman H. Atwater, "Taxation of Churches, Colleges, and Charitable Institutions," *The Princeton Review*, 3, issue 10 (October 1874), p. 341.

1876: When, in the economy of providence, this land was to be purged of human slavery, and when the strength of government of the people by the people for the people was to be demonstrated, the Republican party came into power.

Proceedings of the Republican National Convention, Held at Cincinnati, Ohio, June 14, 15, and 16, 1876, reported by M. A. Clancy (Concord, New Hampshire: Republic Press Association, 1876), p. 55.

1879: The American idea of a republic, as "a government of the people, by the people, and for the people," has been consistently developed and ceased to be a mere experiment.

Philip Schaff, "Progress of Christianity in the United States," *The Princeton Review*, 2 (1879), p. 213.

1879: The Volunteer Soldiers of the Union, whose Valor and Patriotism saved to the world a "Government of the People, by the People, and for the People [a toast]."

Robert G. Ingersoll, "The Grant Banquet. Chicago, November 13, 1879," in *The Works of Robert G. Ingersoll*, ed. by Emmett F. Fields (New York: C. P. Farrell, 1902), p. 81.

1884: President Lincoln defined democracy to be "the government of the people by the people for the people." This is a sufficiently compact statement of it as a political arrangement.

James Russell Lowell, *Democracy and Other Addresses* (Boston: Houghton, Mifflin and Company, 1887), p. 20.

1890: Let us hold fast to the sublime declaration of Lincoln. Let us insist that this, the Republic, is "A government of the people, by the people, and for the people."

Robert G. Ingersoll, "God in the Constitution," in *The Works of Robert G. Ingersoll*, ed. by Emmett F. Fields (New York: C. P. Farrell, 1902), p. 134.

1894: Between the political institutions of the several nations which compose the civilized world there is no gap so great as that which separates those of Russia from those of the United States. Our civil war was fought that "government of

> the people, by the people, for the people should not perish from the earth." In this country there is universal suffrage.
>
> Anonymous, "Against Russian Treaty," *The New York Times* (June 6, 1894), p. 8.

These texts in contexts are all precise citations of the proverbial utterance by Abraham Lincoln. But there are, of course, also other references which are not quite so sacrosanct. For example, Charles Dickens made the following statement during a speech on April 10, 1869, at Liverpool: "It appeared to me [...] that literature was a dignified profession, by which any man might stand or fall. I made a compact with myself that in my person literature should stand, and by itself, of itself, and for itself; and there is no consideration on earth which would induce me to break that bargain" (*The Works of Charles Dickens. Letters and Speeches* (New York: Hearst's International Library, 1893), vol. 2, p. 562). It would be difficult to prove that Dickens is playing here with Lincoln's triad, but the addition of "there is no consideration on earth" also brings to mind Lincoln's "shall not perish from the earth," and thus Dickens might well have been aware of the formula.

Oscar Wilde on the other hand, in his essay on "The Soul of Man Under Socialism" (1895) very obviously negates the meaning of Lincoln's phrase, while he keeps its wording and structure intact:

> *All modes of government are failures.* Despotism is unjust to everybody, including the despot, who was probably made for better things. Oligarchies are unjust to the many, and ochlocracies are unjust to the few. High hopes were once formed of democracy; but democracy means simply the bludgeoning of the people by the people for the people. It has been found out. I must say that it was high time, for all authority is quite degrading.
>
> *The Complete Works of Oscar Wilde* (New York: William H. Wise, 1927), vol. 10, p. 22.

Neither Lincoln nor Douglass would have shared this cynicism about the American experiment in a democratic government. But how pleased would they have been by the following remarks which the civil war soldier, lawyer, orator, and writer Robert G. Ingersoll included in his lecture "Eight to Seven Address" (1877) that dealt with electoral reforms: "We are equals. We are all fellow-citizens. In a Government of the people, by the people and for the people, there shall not be an outcast class, whether white or black"

(*The Works of Robert G. Ingersoll*, ed. by Emmett F. Fields (New York: C. P. Farrell, 1902), vol. 9, p. 256.

It does seem strange, however, that President Grover Cleveland in his First Inaugural Address of March 4, 1885, does not employ the entire triad that must have been on his mind:

> Amid the din or party strife the people's choice was made, but its attendant circumstances have demonstrated anew the strength and safety of a government by the people. In each succeeding year it more clearly appears that our democratic principle needs no apology, and that in its fearless and faithful application is to be found the surest guarantee of good government. [...] This is still the government of all the people, and it should be none the less an object of their affectionate solicitude.
>
> Cited from John Gabriel Hunt (ed.), *The Inaugural Addresses of the Presidents* (New York: Gramercy Books, 1997, p. 244.

But be that as it may, the last words of this review of nineteenth-century appearances of Lincoln's proverb belongs to the women's suffrage leader and social reformer Elizabeth Cady Stanton, who included the following remarks in her "Address of Welcome to the International Council of Women" on March 26, 1888, at Washington, D.C. There is a good chance that Frederick Douglass might have been there for this memorable event, and if so, he would have been most pleased to hear his friend Abraham Lincoln's proverbial words used in this fashion and context:

> Here, under the very shadow of the Capitol of this great nation, whose dome is crowned with the Goddess of Liberty, the women from many lands have assembled at last, to claim their rightful place as equal factors in the great movements of the nineteenth century. So we bid our distinguished guests welcome, thrice welcome to our triumphant democracy. I hope they will be able to stay long enough to take a bird's-eye view of our vast possessions, to see what can be done in a moral, as well as material point of view, in a government of the people. In the Old World they have governments and people; here we have a government of the people, by the people, for the people; that is, we soon shall have when that important half called women are enfranchised, and the laboring masses know how to use the power they possess.
>
> *The Selected Papers of Elizabeth Cady Stanton and Susan B. Anthoiny*, ed. Ann D. Gordon (New Brunswick, New Jersey: Rutgers University Press, 2009), vol. 5, p. 99.

Thirteen years later, in a letter of February 19, 1901, she insisted once again that women should be entitled to vote in a true democracy by slightly misquoting Abraham Lincoln:

> Abraham Lincoln, mid the exciting scenes of our Civil War, at Gettysburg while eulogizing the heroes in that great battle, said: "This is a government of the people, for the people, by the people." Statistics show that women constitute a majority of the people, yet they have no part in the government, no protection under it for their most sacred rights; no voice in the laws or the law makers. It is a pertinent question, are women people? Or are all these great principles glittering generalities – having no application whatever to the majority of the people?
>
> *The Selected Papers of Elizabeth Cady Stanton and Susan B. Anthoiny*, ed. Ann D. Gordon (New Brunswick, New Jersey: Rutgers University Press, 2013), vol. 6, p. 385.

This is indeed effective rhetoric, quoting a well-known Lincoln proverbial phrase in a most positive way and then adding an unexpected twist to it that places it right in the middle of women's rights and the whole problem of voting by women and the masses in general. Abraham Lincoln's proverbial definition of a democratic government has established itself well, and it will be made use of in whatever way to comment on the positive and negative sides of the American government.

The First Half of the Twentieth Century and the "American Creed"

The revealing contextualized texts of the proverb during the nineteenth century recount the struggle of the American society toward a meaningful and sincere interpretation of this democratic wisdom. By the beginning of the twentieth century, the proverb lost its limited male orientation and can in fact be understood as a piece of folk wisdom describing democratic principles where race and gender should not make a difference. This is clearly indicated by a lecture on "The Country's Path to Duty" which Archbishop John Ireland of Chicago delivered on February 13, 1903, to commemorate the ninety-fourth anniversary of the birth of Abraham Lincoln:

> The Republic is what she is because she has vitally remained what Washington intended her to be, what Lincoln bade her to be – a government of the people, by the people, for the people. This is what she must remain, if she is still to live and to reign. The vital principles of democracy must animate her. Every man under the flag must be equal before the law in civil and political rights; it matters not what his place of birth, what his religious creed, what the color of his face; if he is an American citizen, the laws of the land must shield him, the favors of the land must flow upon him.
>
> Archbishop John Ireland, "The Country's Path of Duty," *The New York Times* (February 13, 1903), p. 1.

In the same year, on October 31, 1903, President Theodore Roosevelt made the following Thanksgiving Proclamation, proudly quoting the words of Lincoln without having to name the former president. His fellow citizens knew very well whom he was citing: "In no other place and at no other time has the experiment of government of the people, by the people, for the people been tried on so vast a scale as here in our own country in the opening years of the twentieth century. Failure would not only be a dreadful thing for us, but a dreadful thing for all mankind, because it would mean loss of hope for all who believe in the power and righteousness of liberty" ("A Proclamation," *The New York Times* (November 1, 1903), p. 11). A little over one month later Roosevelt included the following paragraph in his "Third Annual Message" of December 7, 1903, in which he changed the end of the Gettysburg Adress without referring to Lincoln to a negative vision in order to strengthen his argument against bribery:

> There can be no crime more serious than bribery. Other offenses violate one law while corruption strikes at the foundation of all law. Under our form of Government all authority is vested in the people and by them delegated to those who represent them in official capacity. There can be no offense heavier than that of him in whom such a sacred trust has been reposed, who sells it for his own gain and enrichment; and no less heavy is the offense of the bribe giver. He is worse than the thief, for the thief robs the individual, while the corrupt official plunders an entire city or State. He is as wicked as the murderer, for the murderer may only take one life against the law, while the corrupt official and the man who corrupts the official alike aim at the assassination of the commonwealth itself. Government of the people, by the people, for the people will perish from the face of the earth if bribery is tolerated. The givers

> and takers of bribes stand on an evil preeminence of infamy. The exposure and punishment of public corruption is an honor to a nation, not a disgrace.
>
> *The Works of Theodore Roosevelt. Memorial Edition* (New York: Charles Scribner's Sons, 1925), vol. 17, p. 209.

Roosevelt urged the American people "to war steadfastly for good and against all the forces of evil, public and private," so that it might never come to the collapse of the democratic government, as Ambrose Bierce expressed it in his satirical text of October 17, 1904: "Opposition, *n*. In politics the party that prevents the Government from running amuck by hamstringing it – One day a bill imposing a tax on warts was defeated – the members of the Government party had not been nailed to their seats! This so enraged the King that the Prime Minister was put to death, the parliament was dissolved with a battery of artillery, and government of the people, by the people, for the people perished from [the fictional] Ghargaroo" (*The Unabridged Devil's Dictionary*, ed. by David E. Schultz and S. T. Joshi (Athens, Georgia: University of Georgia Press, 2002), pp. 174–175). With World War I raging in Europe and endangering democratic governments, the *New York Times* published a list of demands on December 24, 1916, "which Americans of Anglo-Saxon blood would like to see made by England to Germany." As expected, one of the requests included the basic proverb of democracy: "England believes in the principle that the government of a nation rests on the consent of the governed: that government of the many by the few must come to an end, and that government of the people by the people for the people must take its place" (*The New York Times* (December 24, 1916), p. X8). Half a year later, at the heights of World War I, former President Roosevelt made a similar statement in an essay of June 1917 entitled "Uncle Sam's Only Friend is Uncle Sam":

> The United States has – and deserves to have – only one friend in the world. This is the United States. We have ourselves treated the Hague Conventions as scraps of paper; and we cannot expect any one else to show the respect for such treaties which we have lacked. Our safety and therefore safety of democratic institutions rests on our own strength and only on our own strength. If we are a true democracy, if we really believe in government of the people by the people and for the people, if we believe in social and industrial justice to be achieved through the people, and therefore in the right of the people to demand the service of all the people,

> let us make the Army fundamentally an army of the whole people. This will be carrying out the democratic ideal.
>
> *Newer Roosevelt Messages. Speeches, Letters and Magazine articles Dealing with the War, Before and After, and Other Vital Topics*, ed. William Griffith (New York: The Current Literature Publishing Company, 1919), vol. 3, pp. 845–846 (the entire essay on pp. 840–847)

Theodore Roosevelt was clearly arguing during wartime that all Americans needed to step up for service of all kinds so that the American democracy could survive. Franklin D. Roosevelt would use similar rhetoric during World War II to mobilize Americans into action for the sake of saving democracy.

In any case, the First World Wat ended with the armistice day of November 11, 1918. In the political fervor of the day, an interesting occurrence took place in the United States House of Representatives on April 6, 1918, when its members adopted the little-known *The American's Creed*, formulated by William Tyler Page, a veteran House of Representatives employee from Friendship Heights, Maryland. In March, 1917, the city of Baltimore had offered a prize of $1000 in a contest of formulating a national creed. Several thousand creeds were submitted, and no. 384 by Page was selected:

> *The American's Creed*
>
> I believe in the United States of America as a Government of the people, by the people, for the people, whose just powers are derived from the consent of the governed; a democracy in a Republic; a sovereign Nation of many sovereign States; a perfect Union, one and inseparable; established upon those principles of freedom, equality, justice, and humanity for which American patriots sacrificed their lives and fortunes.
>
> I therefore believe it is my duty to my country to love it, to support its Constitution, to obey its laws, to respect its flag, and to defend it against all enemies.
>
> *Congressional Record, Containing the Proceedings and Debates of the Second Session of the Sixty-Fifth Congress of the United States of America* (Washington, D.C.: Government Printing Office, 1918), vol. 56, p. 4745.

While the text and report concerning the creed occupies about a third of a column in the *Congressional Record*, much more space was allotted to it (five large columns) in the *Appendix to the Congressional Record* (see "The American's Creed" in *Congressional Record, Appendix and Index to Parts 1-11 of The Proceedings and Debates of the Second Session of the Sixty-Fifth Congress of the United States of America* (Washington, D.C.: Government Printing Office, 1918), vol. 56, part 12, pp. 286–289). There is a detailed discussion by Dr. Claxton, United States Commissioner of Education, of the various quotations of important historical American documents which Page assembled into his collage, including "that the second clause – 'A government of the people, by the people, for the people' – is from the preamble to the Constitution of the United States [incorrect!], Daniel Webster's speech in the Senate of January 26, 1830, and Abraham Lincoln's Gettysburg speech" (Ibid. p. 287 (left column). There is also this somewhat longer comment: "The power of condensation of language is one of the most valuable in writing or speaking. That is the reason why this creed that he [Page] has written will be popular. It contains everything that is necessary, and there are no wasted words in it. He has Lincoln's most famous phrase, one that will live forever, that can not be amended. And it is strange to remember how close Daniel Webster came to getting that phrase. Webster said this was a government of all the people, by all the people, for all the people, and all that Lincoln did to it was to leave out the superfluous word 'all,' thereby making it immortal" (Ibid., p. 287 (right column). Speaker Clark of the House, who made these remarks, is, of course mistaken in his quotation of Daniel Webster, who, on January 26, 1830, had said (as discussed above): "It is the people's Constitution, the people's government, made for the people, made by the people, and answerable to the people." It was in fact Theodore Parker and not Lincoln, who (as pointed out above) on May 29, 1850, had spoken of "[...] a democracy, that is, a government of all the people, by all the people, for all the people." As the record stands, the *Congressional Record* is wrong, and in regard to the discussion of Daniel Webster's use of the phrase above, it should also be added that the adjective "all" is not as superfluous as Speaker Clark might have thought. It behooves us even today to stress that we do indeed mean government of each and every citizen when we quote Lincoln's version of the definition of democracy. At the end of the proceedings, Commissioner of Education Claxton made this final comment that was greeted with applause: "With the consent of those who have these proceedings in charge, I consider it my duty to see that every schoolhouse in the United States is furnished with a copy of this creed, to be learned by the 20,000,000 people now in these schoolhouses and the scores and hundreds of millions who will follow" (Ibid., p. 288 (left column). At the very end of this report, *The American's Creed* was read aloud as Tyler Page was presented to the entire House that cheered him with applause (Ibid., p. 289 (left column). However, these emotions with all their patriotism also reflect war times, and the fate of the creed was not as favorable as these proceedings might suggest. I don't know whether the creed was ever mailed to the schools and whether millions of students did learn it by heart. In any case, *The American's Creed* has not become part and parcel of American cultural literacy and has vanished from the landscape. It must be remembered that today the practice at schools to have students memorize the preamble to the Constitution or at least parts of the Declaration of Independence or Gettysburg Address is also waning, a cultural process that carries definite problems with it. These national treasures should well remain in the minds and hearts of all American citizens as symbols of a free society.

Not many years later Vice President Calvin Coolidge echoed the sentiments expressed in "The American's Creed" in a short speech entitled "The Destiny of America" on May 30, 1923:

> Patriotism is easy to understand in America. It means looking out for yourself by looking out for your country. In no other nation on earth does this principle have such complete application. It comes most naturally from the fundamental doctrine of our land that the people are supreme. Lincoln stated the substance of the whole matter in his famous phrase, "government of the people, by the people, and for the people." The authority of the law here is not something which is imposed upon the people; it is the will of the people themselves. The decision of the court here is not something which is apart from the people; it is the judgment of the people themselves. The right of the ownership of property here is not something withheld from the people; it is the privilege of the people themselves. Their sovereignty is absolute and complete. A definition of the relationship between the institutions of our government and the American people entirely justifies the assertion that: "All things were made by *them*; and without *them* was not anything made that was made." It is because the American government is the sole creation and possession of the people that they have always cherished it and defended it, and always will.
>
> Calvin Coolidge, *The Price of Freedom. Speeches and Addresses* (New York: C. Scribner's Sons, 1924, p. 333.

As will be shown later, American presidents delight on calling on Lincoln's proverbial triad as a democratic principle. More often than not, they cite it together with the president's name, thus keeping the memory of its origin during the Civil War alive.

This issue of memory was part of a column on the "Topics of the Times" in *The New York Times* of December 4, 1936, where a commentator thought it well to remember Lincoln's famous words on the basics of democracy as the dictatorial Nazi regime in Germany was gaining ever more threatening momentum:

> The new Nazi critic will conclude with a few words about an American literary masterpiece, the Gettysburg Address. This is approximately 250 [272!] words long and was delivered on Nov. 19, 1863, on the site of the battlefield of Gettysburg, a borough and the county seat of Adams County, Pa., thirty-five miles southwest of Harrisburg. The speech was delivered by ABRAHAM LINCOLN, who was then 54 years old and 6 feet 4 inches in height. He was the sixteenth President of the United States.
>
> The reason why the Gettysburg Address is so close to the hearts of all Americans is that they can never remember whether it is of the people, for the people, by the people, or by the people, of the people, for the people, or for the people, by the people, of the people. This compels them to look up the original text and has made the speech near and dear to them.
>
> *The New York Times* (December 4, 1936), p. 24.

The author of this satirical paragraph never gets the triad "of the people, by the people, for the people" quite right, but that is, quite surely, the point of the exercise. The indirect message of these comments is clearly that Americans ought to recall their impressive history of valiant struggles for freedom and liberty at a time when a serious menace is threatening Europe and the world.

In the same year the American poet and renowned Lincoln biographer Carl Sandburg stepped forth with his epic poem *The People, Yes* (1936), celebrating America as a country of immigrants, diversity, and nevertheless national unity. The impressive section on Abraham Lincoln, quoting freely from his works, includes the following lines:

> Lincoln?
> He was a mystery in smoke and flags
> saying yes to the smoke, yes to the flags,

> yes to the paradoxes of democracy,
> yes to the hopes of government
> of the people by the people for the people,
> no to debauchery of the public mind,
> no to personal malice nursed and fed,
> yes to the Constitution when a help,
> no to the Constitution when a hindrance,
> yes to man as a struggler amid illusions,
> each man fated to answer for himself:
> Which of the faiths and illusions of mankind
> must I choose for my own sustaining light
> to bring me beyond the present wilderness?
> Carl Sandburg, *The People, Yes* (New York: Harcourt, Brace and Company, 1936), p. 134 (section 57, pp. 134–139, of the poem is a tribute to Lincoln).

And yet, not every literary appearance of Lincoln's proverb is cast in a positive light. In Michael Arlen's novel *The Flying Dutchman* (1939), for example, things are seen in a rather cynical way: "We say that those dictatorships [Mussolini, Stalin, and Hitler] make free people servile. But the fact remains that the enormous wealth of people like ourselves [leaders of industry] is due to that servile rottenness inherent in the democratic system which we call the government of the people, for the people, by the people, and to hell with the people" (Michael Arlen, *The Flying Dutchman* (New York: Doubleday, Doran & Company, 1939). p. 187). In light of modern concerns along these lines, it is surprising that the addition of "to hell with the people" does not appear more frequently in oral and written communication.

Lincoln's words also reappeared in the mass media of the turbulent years of the first half of the twentieth century with its two world wars, prohibition, stock market crash, and many social problems. At times, the famed proverb is parodied to add satirical bite to the critical comments:

> 1923: America is still a government of the naïve, for the naïve, and by the naïve. He who does not know this, nor relish it, has no inkling of the nature of his country.
>
> Christopher Morley, *Inward Ho!* (Garden City, New York: Doubleday, Page & Company, 1923), pp. 41–42.
>
> 1924: They [the two major political parties] have fallen under control of a single dominant power which uses them to further its own interests. Instead of a government of the people, by the people, for the people, we have a government of

Wall Street, by Wall Street and for Wall Street. I [Senator Wheeler of Montana, Vice Presidential candidate on the La Follette ticket] use the term "Wall Street" to designate the industrial and commercial interests centering in that crooked line in lower New York City.

Anonymous, "Wheeler Condemns Both Old Parties," in *The New York Times* (September 2, 1924), p. 3.

1928: Voters of the U.S.A. – Wanted all 100 per cent citizens to support the Progressive Party, advocating the wisdom of a non-political Government of the people, by the people, for the people; the initiative, the referendum and the recall is the answer to the prohibition problem and business and social unrest, with equity and justice purges of bigotry.

John Clinton McGee, "Public Notice," *The New York Times* (September 2, 1928), p. 19.

1939: One specific service which a program of education for democracy can render is to bring back into common use an old synonym for democracy, and that is the word "freedom." The connotations of democracy are precious, and the issues between the democratic nations and their avowed enemies in the world today are sufficiently clear. Yet there is a warmth about the thing called freedom that makes the heart beat faster. Democracy is technically a way of government, but freedom is a way of life. American pulses respond easily to the ideal of government of the people, by the people, for the people. But a free people comes even closer to us than a self-governing people, except as the mind automatically translates a self-governing people into a nation of freemen.

Anonymous, "Democracy is Freedom," *The New York Times* (August 13, 1939), p. E8.

1940: Since the Declaration of Independence the United States has adhered to some form of democracy, which Lincoln said meant "government of the people, by the people, for the people." Such government has always been characteristic of this country. Whether it "can long endure" is being challenged. If it cannot, it will because the American Way has been discarded.

M. Fellows, "The American Way Viewed as Heritage to Be Guarded," *The New York Times* ((September 1, 1940), p. E7 (letter to the editor).

1943: So – we say that so long as the spirit of man shall not perish from the earth, government of the people, for the people, by the people, will not perish. The question presented is this: Shall we go through the misery and suffering of re-creating our own country after this war, or shall we hold tenaciously to

> what, from past sufferings, we have learned to be the best form of government for us that we could have devised?
>
> Julis Henry Cohen, "'Government of the People, by the People, for the People' … Shall It Perish?" *American Bar Association Journal*, 29 (1943), pp. 3–7.
>
> 1943: How do Abraham Lincoln's three [the other two are "You can fool some of the people ..." and "The Lord must love the plain people ..."] best-known discoveries stand up on his 134th birthday? Only a year ago we would have had to say that the outlook was grim. Government of the people, by the people, for the people had ceased to exist on the continent of Europe. The world's two great democracies, Britain and ourselves, were fighting for survival, with the prospect of victory none too bright. If the English-speaking peoples went down it would be all over with free government. The test which had been successfully met at Gettysburg would have been annulled eighty years later. Now that we are sure of victory for the United Nations we are justified in saying that when the present job is finished Abraham Lincoln will be more than vindicated.
>
> Anonymous, "Topics of the Times," *The New York Times* (February 13, 1943), p. 10.

The last few paragraphs show how Abraham Lincoln's words became a rallying cry in America's war with Nazi Germany. It was indeed a very positive propagandistic use of the proverb, one that helped to convince the American population that the menace and horror of the Hitler regime had to be eliminated. To this end, President Franklin D. Roosevelt proclaimed that May 21, 1944, be "I Am an American Day." For the special celebration of this day, the Immigration and Naturalization Service of the Department of Justice issued a manual for "The Gateway to Citizenship" which included various documents in the form of speeches, songs, prayers, etc. for a better understanding of the democratic principles of the United States. *The New York Times* printed a page of excerpts from various texts by George Washington, James Madison, Ralph Waldo Emerson, William Tyler Page, Stephen Vincent Benét, Henry Cabot Lodge, Albert Einstein, and others under the headline "'I Am an American': A Creed and a Code" in *The New York Times* (May 21, 1944), p. SM16. Among them in the first position is *The American's Credo* by William Tyler Page discussed above, thus giving this patriotic statement an important public forum after all.

The Rhetoric of Two World Leaders: Roosevelt and Churchill

Both Franklin D. Roosevelt and Winston S. Churchill made repeated use of Abraham Lincoln's proverbial triad, with Churchill even having a bit of fun with it in the House of Commons on April 28, 1927, when he was accused of wrong appropriations for the road fund. Rejecting such accusations, he stated that he was tired of having to deal with such problems as "Government of the motorists, by the motorists, for the motorists" (*Winston S. Churchill: His Complete Speeches 1897–1963*, ed. Robert Rhodes James (New York: Chelsea House Publishers, 1974), vol. 4, p. 4208) and that he was not going to fight this battle any longer. He also alluded to the phrase in the satirical title of the essay "Government of the by the for the Dole-Drawers" (1931), restating it more fully in the text itself: "'Government of the dole-drawers, by the dole-drawers, for the dole-drawers'" (*The Collected Essays of Sir Winston Churchill: Churchill and Politics*, ed. Michael Wolff (London: Library of Imperial History, 1976), vol. 2, pp. 218 and 220). This varied triad was directed against the financial and unemployment policies by the Labor Government in England, but things became much more serious for this masterful orator as Hitler's regime grew in power. In his essay "I Ask You – What Price Freedom?" (1936) he states straight-forwardly what the task at hand is:

> These are not the days when the ordinary citizen can afford to neglect any precaution or withhold any labour or sacrifice which is necessary to preserve the health and strength of Parliamentary institutions or to uphold, in the famous American expression, "government of the people, by the people, for the people". We will not surrender these title deeds of individual rights for which uncounted generations of illustrious men and women have fought and conquered to the morbid regimentation of a totalitarian State, whether it be pressed upon us by force from without or by conspiracy from within.
>
> *The Collected Essays of Sir Winston Churchill: Churchill and the War*, ed. Michael Wolff (London: Library of Imperial History, 1976), vol. 1, p. 361.

When as Prime Minister he traveled to the United States to deliver his speech on "A Long and Hard War" to a Joint Session of Congress on December 26, 1941, he included the following personal remarks in the second paragraph of this memorable address:

> I have been in full harmony all my life with the tides which have flowed on both sides of the Atlantic against privilege and monopoly, and I have steered confidently towards the Gettysburg ideal of "government of the people by the people for the people." I owe my advancement entirely to the House of Commons, whose servant I am. In my country, as in yours, public men are proud to be the servants of the State and would be ashamed to be its masters. On any day, if they thought the people wanted it, the House of Commons could by a simple vote remove me from my office. But I am not worrying about it at all. As a matter of fact, I am sure they will approve very highly of my journey here, for which I obtained the King's permission in order to meet the President of the United States and to arrange with him all that mapping-out of our military plans, and for all those intimate meetings of the high officers of the armed services of both countries, which are indispensable to the successful prosecution of the war.
>
> *Winston S. Churchill: His Complete Speeches 1897–1963*, ed. Robert Rhodes James (New York: Chelsea House Publishers, 1974), vol. 6, pp. 6536–6537.

Americans obviously were pleased with this nod to Lincoln and the ideal of a democratic government. And Churchill was not merely doing lip-service, he meant what he said and repeated this political maxim in his "Review of the War" on January 18, 1945, in the House of Commons in London when the war was slowly but surely drawing to an end:

> We have one principle about the liberated countries or the repentant satellite countries which we strive for according to the best of our ability and resources. Here is the principle. I will state it in the broadest and most familiar terms: Government of the people, by the people, for the people, set up on a basis of election by free and universal suffrage, with secrecy of the ballot and no intimidation. That is and has always been the policy of this Government in all countries. This is our only aim, our only interest, and our only care. It is to that goal that we try to make our way across all the difficulties, obstacles and perils of the long road.
>
> *Winston S. Churchill: His Complete Speeches 1897–1963*, ed. Robert Rhodes James (New York: Chelsea House Publishers, 1974), vol. 7, p. 7084.

Lincoln would surely have been proud of this policy of "malice towards none" based on democratic principles. Two days after the end of World War II, Churchill rose again on August 16, 1945, in the House of Commons to deliver his prophetic speech on "The Iron Curtain Begins to Fall (Final Review of the War)" that looked into the future of a Europe divided into East and West. With clear understanding of the political challenges that were facing Western Europe, he returned one more time to the proverbial triad that had served him so well before:

> We must know where we stand, and we must make clear where we stand, in these affairs of the Balkans and of Eastern Europe [with Russia taking control], and indeed of any country which comes into this field. Our ideal is government of the people, by the people, for the people – the people being free without duress to express, by secret ballot without intimidation, their deep-seated wish as to the form and conditions of the Government under which they are to live.
>
> *Winston S. Churchill: His Complete Speeches 1897–1963*, ed. Robert Rhodes James (New York: Chelsea House Publishers, 1974), vol. 7, p. 7214.

It is, of course, an impressive tribute to American values for Winston S. Churchill, as Prime Minister of Great Britain and Americanophile, to cite this special proverb in his key speeches regarding world politics. On the American side of the struggle of World War II. it was, of course, Franklin D. Roosevelt with his rhetorical prowess that made use of Lincoln's proverbial triad. Still as Governor of the state of New York he cited merely two-thirds of it as a description of the American democracy in a speech of January 17, 1930:

> We speak lightly of this being the era of Democracy without realizing what a tremendous change has been brought about, or how it has revolutionized the everyday existence of every one of us. In this building up of a theory of government "by the people, for the people" our country has been the leader of the civilized nations of the world, and I think I can proudly add that our State has been the leader in our country.
>
> *The Public Papers and Addresses of Franklin D. Roosevelt, 1928–1932* (New York: Random House, 1938), vol. 1, p. 330.

Barely two months later, on March 2, 1930, he did cite the entire triad as an effective appeal for democratic principles as a stronghold against developments toward an autocracy of the privileged and commercial interests:

> A lack of study and knowledge of the matter of sovereign power of the people through State government has led us to drift insensibly toward that dangerous disregard of minority needs which marks the beginning of the autocracy. Let us not forget that there can be an autocracy of special classes or commercial

interests which is utterly incompatible with a real democracy whose boasted motto is, "of the people, by the people and for the people."

The Public Papers and Addresses of Franklin D. Roosevelt, 1928–1932 (New York: Random House, 1938), vol. 1, 571.

In a speech of August 31, 1939, just one day before the start of the Second World War, he spoke in high praise of the accomplishments of his presidential administration by rephrasing Lincoln's "people"-triad with the word "democracy" for a special affect in opposition to the dictatorships abroad:

These are material gains of which we may well be proud and they have been accompanied since 1933 by such social advances as are embodied in the Social Security program, for which this and future generations will always be thankful.

They have been accomplished in a democracy, for a democracy and by a democracy and they can only be retained and expanded through a continuation of the principles and practices to which we as a Nation have always been committed and which we are determined shall be unchanged.

The Public Papers and Addresses of Franklin D. Roosevelt, 1939 (New York: Random House, 1941), vol. 8, p. 356.

During the war there is also the following statement of March 20, 1942 by President Roosevelt with which he made clear by way of recalling Abraham Lincoln's proverbial words that the American soldiers were fighting Nazi Germany in the name of democratic ideals:

Never before in the one hundred and sixty-six years of our history as a free Republic under God have our armed forces had so much meaning for us all. We are engaged in our greatest war, a war that will leave none of our lives wholly untouched.

We shall win that war as we have won every war we have fought. We are fighting it with a combined force of free men that is, in Lincoln's words, of the people, by the people, for the people of the United States of America.

The Public Papers and Addresses of Franklin D. Roosevelt, 1942 (New York: Harper & Brothers, 1950), vol. 11, p. 181.

It is interesting to note that while Roosevelt relied quite heavily on known quotations, including Lincoln's "that these dead shall not have died in vain" from the Gettysburg Address" and "with malice towards none, with charity for all" of Lincoln's Second Inaugural Address of March 4, 1865, he did not make any further use of Lincoln's proverbial triad that became a leitmotif for his successor Harry S. Truman.

President Harry S. Truman's Proverbial Preoccupation

Following the death of Franklin D. Roosevelt and in the aftermath of the Second World War, it was Harry S. Truman who repeatedly drew on Lincoln's wisdom to underscore the ideals of a democratic government. On March 29, 1941, he stated the abbreviated form of the proverb during a "Speech on 'Jackson Day'" in Louisville, Kentucky: "He [President Andrew Jackson] did not set up a government of, by, and for the people but he did force a government to respond to the voice of the people. He did not solve all of the problems of his age, but he did and does inspire us to believe that problems can and must be solved" (*Congressional Record*, vol. 87, part 11 (1941), p. A1528). The same formulation was repeated in an undelivered draft speech of October 1946 dealing with the vexing problem of price control after the war. He was, in fact, venting his frustration in the following comments: "You've deserted your President for a mess of pottage, a piece of beef – a side of bacon. My fellow citizens, *you* are the government. This is a government of, by and for the people. If you the people insist on following Mammon instead of Almighty God – your President can't stop you all by himself. He can only lead you to peace and happiness with your consent and your willing cooperation" (*Off the Record: The Private Papers of Harry S. Truman*, ed. by Robert H. Ferrell (New York: Harper & Row, 1980), p. 102). This is a fine example of Truman as President scolding his people for not seeing the right path toward economic improvement – "giving them hell," as it were (for Truman's ability to use strong language see Eldorous L. Dayton, *Give 'em Hell Harry. An Informal Biography of the Terrible Tempered Mr. T.* (New York: The Devin-Adair Company, 1956); and Mark Goodman (ed.), *Give 'em Hell, Harry* (New York: Award Books, 1974).

During his presidential campaign in the fall of 1948, President Truman crisscrossed the country by train and made dozens of so-called "whistle-stops" in small towns. He would stand on the rear platform of a railroad car and do a few minutes worth of plain talking with the country people, referring again and again to Lincoln's proverbial definition of a democratic government. As will become obvious from the following five excerpts, Truman once in a while got the order of the prepositions mixed up in the heat of the campaign rhetoric:

> I am fighting for the education of the people of this country. When you have the proper education, you can't help but believe that our system of Government [in opposition to that of the Communists] is the best that's ever been conceived in the history of the world. It's a Government of the people [Truman did not complete the triad in this case]. In fact, you are the Government. You are the Government, and you are the Government because you have a right of free franchise, and when you don't exercise that right of free franchise, you are not doing the right thing by your country. You are a shirker, and when things don't go right in your Government and you don't vote, you're to blame for it.
>
> Porvo, Utah; September 21, 1948; *Public Papers of the Presidents of the United States: Harry S. Truman*. January 1 to December 31, 1948 (Washington, D.C.: U.S. Government Printing Office, 1964), p. 527.
>
> Now they're [the Republicans] trying to get out of that [raising money to deal with cattle diseases]. They go around telling you just exactly how they feel toward the people and what they'll do for the people. I wish you'd go back over the list of things that they did to the people in the 80th [so-called "do-nothing"] Congress. You wouldn't have one bit of trouble making up your mind. I know the people of Texas are going to make up their minds the right way because they know what's what when it comes to Government of the people, for the people, and by the people. I'm asking you to turn out at election day and give us the biggest majority we've ever had in the history of the country.
>
> Marfa, Texas; September 25, 1948; *Public Papers of the Presidents of the United States: Harry S. Truman*. January 1 to December 31, 1948 (Washington, D.C.: U.S. Government Printing Office, 1964), p. 571.
>
> I want all of you to vote this time, and then I know that the country will be in safe hands, because when the people are aroused and when the people know what the issues are we have never had any difficulty making this Government run in the interests of the people, for the people, and by the people. I am going all up and down this country telling you that your interests and my interests and the interests of all the people are at stake in this campaign.

Oneida, New York; October 8, 1948; *Public Papers of the Presidents of the United States: Harry S. Truman*. January 1 to December 31, 1948 (Washington, D.C.: U.S. Government Printing Office, 1964), p. 708.

I want you to think just how out of place Lincoln would be with present day Republicans. Republicans don't charge low fees [as Lincoln did as a lawyer] any longer. The higher the better is their motto. They don't think any longer about "of the people, by the people, and for the people." The record of the Republican 80th Congress is proof of that.

Danville, Illinois; October 12, 1948; *Public Papers of the Presidents of the United States: Harry S. Truman*. January 1 to December 31, 1948 (Washington, D.C.: U.S. Government Printing Office, 1964), pp. 753–754.

Now I want to say this to you, that if you believe in government of, by, and for the people, if you believe in your own self-interest, the best thing for you to do on November the 2nd is to go to the polls early and vote the straight democratic ticket, and then the country will be safe for another 4 years.

New York City, New York; October 28, 1948; *Public Papers of the Presidents of the United States: Harry S. Truman*. January 1 to December 31, 1948 (Washington, D.C.: U.S. Government Printing Office, 1964), p. 903.

Truman did well in relying on the democratic proverb for his reelection campaign. Lincoln's words served him well to spread his grass-root message, and he continued citing the words of his revered Abraham Lincoln during the next four years in office. In his "Remarks to Officers of the Veterans of Foreign Wars" on February 18, 1949, he employed it once again: "I am counting on you for help and support to carry out those policies which will make the country a better place in which to live and one which will give the rest of the world an example of how a government, of and by and for the people, can function" (*Public Papers of the Presidents of the United States: Harry S. Truman*. January 1 to December 31, 1949 (Washington, D.C.: U.S. Government Printing Office, 1964), p. 140). He made similar "Remarks to Members of the Reserve Officers Association" on June 28, 1950: "I believe that this is a Government of and by and for the people, as Abraham Lincoln said. And as far as I can, as President of the United States, I am trying to implement that theory, not only in the United States but in the world at large" (*Public Papers of the Presidents of the United States: Harry S. Truman*. January

1 to December 31, 1950 (Washington, D.C.: U.S. Government Printing Office, 1965), p. 497.

These comments, albeit indirectly, indicate Truman's vexing problem with European politics after the war in particular. The so-called "Iron Curtain" had come down to separate Democracy from Communism, and the Cold War also had its start. Truman dealt with these problems more directly in his "Remarks to Members of the Associated Church Press" on March 28, 1951, challenging the other side to be open and forthcoming:

> Our Government is a government of the people, for the people, and by the people, and we are trying to make it work as best we can. And we are making it work. What we want to do is to convince the people behind the Iron Curtain that we do not, under any circumstances, want to control or tell them what to do. All we want is for them – for their own welfare and benefit – to do the things that are necessary for the welfare of their own people, and to do it in their own way. Raise the curtain, and let us see how they do it. Maybe they can teach us something. I know we can teach them something, if they will come and look at us. But they won't come and make the effort to implement the mobilization of the moral forces of the world – all of them – against the unmoral forces. Then we will have peace in the world. And that's all we are striving for. That's all in the world we are striving for.
>
> *Public Papers of the Presidents of the United States: Harry S. Truman*. January 1 to December 31, 1951 (Washington, D.C.: U.S. Government Printing Office, 1965), p. 200.

While Truman once again mixed up his prepositions in this significant passage – one is reminded of President Ronald Reagan's remark some 40 years later on June 12, 1987 at the Berlin Wall: "Mr. Gorbachev, open this gate! Mr. Gorbachev, tear down this wall!" (*Public Papers of the Presidents of the United States: Ronald Reagan*, 1 January to 3 July 1987 (Washington, D.C.: U.S. Government Printing Office, 1989), p. 635) – he certainly gets them straight in an "Address at the Ceremonies Commemorating the 175th Anniversary of the Declaration of Independence" on July 4, 1951, at the Washington Monument. Praising the soldiers who have died in the service for their country, he stated: "They died in order that 'government of the people, by the people, for the people, shall not perish from the earth.' They have died in order that other men might have peace" (*Public Papers of the Presidents of the United States:*

Harry S. Truman. January 1 to December 31, 1951 (Washington, D.C.: U.S. Government Printing Office, 1965), p. 371). Truman is employing a direct quotation from the Gettysburg Address in this case, and as a well-informed historian, having written essays on numerous U.S. presidents (see Margaret Truman (ed.), *Where the Buck Stops. The Personal and Private Writings of Harry S. Truman* (New York: Warner Books, 1989), he checked his source or paid special attention to get it right at this occasion.

This is, however, not the case in a private diary entry written down in Paris on June 6, 1956: "We drove out of Paris at 10 A.M. and arrived at Versailles to see the palace and the gardens. It is the extravaganza of King Louis XIV, the 'Grand Monarque,' whose statement "'I am the State' is one of the historical sentences expressing the Bourbon attitude toward government. It is the exact opposite of 'Government of the people, for the people and by the people,' the statement of Abraham Lincoln" (*Off the Record. The Private Papers of Harry S. Truman*, ed. Robert H. Ferrell (New York: Harper and Row, 1980), p. 333). And finally, there is this short paragraph in a letter of January 31, 1960, that Truman never mailed to Joseph Clark. It shows that the aging former President is still very much involved with party politics, relying one more time on the shortened but correctly cited triad by his idol Abraham Lincoln: "The democratic Party has been the only political party since 1808 that has had the ordinary man's interest in its concept of what government is for. That has been true through Jackson, Lincoln (who coined the phrase 'Of, by and for the people'), Grover Cleveland in his first term, Teddy Roosevelt, to some extent, Woodrow Wilson and Franklin Roosevelt (without reservation)" (*Strictly Personal and Confidential: The Letters Harry Truman Never Mailed*, ed. by Monte M. Poen (Boston: Little, Brown and Company, 1982), p. 133). All of this is "plain talk" in its best sense, and Abraham Lincoln most assuredly would have approved of the way Harry S. Truman used his proverb to advance democratic "government[s] of the people, by the people, for the people" throughout the world.

The "People"-Proverb in the Second Half of the Twentieth Century

During these five decades, Lincoln's proverb has found continued use as a well-known verbal symbol of democracy. At times the name of Abraham

Lincoln is mentioned in order to add his authoritative voice to an argument or observation, but perhaps more often than not it suffices to state the entire phrase by itself or even just to allude to it. While the triad is often employed to comment on governmental issues, it is also called upon to deal with other political and social matters. This is the case, for example, with its effective use in an article on "Our Faith Is Mightier Than Our Atom Bomb" (1949) by David E. Lilienthal, member of the Atomic Energy Commission:

> We should boast, as Whitman would, that the song of America is a song of great horizons; of a "new order of the ages"; of a new way of life under the sun. We should boast that in the United States we have created the most luminous concepts of the objectives of human society that any people has ever dedicated itself to: "life, liberty and the pursuit of happiness"; "government of the people, by the people, for the people"; "We hold these truths to be self-evident, that all men are created equal ... one nation, indivisible, with liberty and justice for all." We in America have no need for slogans of other lands when on our banner are inscribed such imperishable cries of the human spirit as these.
>
> *The New York Times* (March 6, 1949), p. SM11.

With the Cold War in full swing, weapons of mass destruction were very much under discussion, especially in the aftermath of the employment of the atomic bomb. The Soviet Union and the United States started to throw aggressive slogans at each other, and the arms race was well on its way. But what Lilienthal is saying here by way of a number of famous American proverbial quotations is that no such military rhetoric is necessary if the faith of the American people remains strongly embedded in democratic principles. But there were also those voices that questioned the claim of the universality of such American quotations, as was done by E.L. Woodward in his article "Words Loom Large in the World Struggle: Their Meanings Can be Dangerously Elusive" in the *New York Times* of March 16, 1952: "Examine the best known definition of democracy: government of the people, by the people, for the people. Government by what people? Those 'chosen by election'?" (*The New York Times* (March 16, 1952), p. 56). Such a question may serve as a fitting transition to the following contextualized references from the more recent presidents of the United States.

President Dwight D. Eisenhower began his "Proclamation on Citizenship Day and Constitution Week" on June 20, 1958, with a well-chosen introductory reference to the proverbial triad as an underlying principle of democracy:

> Whereas our government of the people, by the people, and for the people is cherished by all American citizens; and
>
> Whereas this government is guaranteed by the Constitution of the United States of America, signed at Philadelphia on September 17, 1787, and secured by the travail. stamina and wisdom of American patriots; and
>
> Whereas it is ever imperative that all our citizens, both native-born and naturalized, understand the significance of this great document so that they may give life and meaning to its principles; [...]
>
> Now, therefore, I, Dwight D. Eisenhower, President of the United States, call upon the appropriate officials of the Government to display the flag of the United States on all Government buildings on Citizenship Day, September 17, 1958; and I urge Federal, State, and local officials, as well as all religious, civic, educational and other organizations, to arrange for appropriate ceremonies on Citizenship Day to strengthen a better understanding of our rights and our responsibilities as citizens of the United States.
>
> https://www.presidency.ucsb.edu/documents/proclamation-3247-citizenship-day-and-constitution-week-1958

After this civic call to all the people Eisenhower cited Lincoln's final phrase of the Gettysburg Address once again about one year later on August 6, 1959, in a radio and television address on "Congressional Bills for Labor Reform," referring quite directly to the question of what makes a democratic government:

> Nearly one hundred years ago Abraham Lincoln in his memorable address spoke of the sacrifices made so that in his words: "Government of the people, by the people, for the people shall not perish from the earth." That was the question he posed to our nation in his generation. In our lives and actions, the people of America, in private and public sectors, daily face millions of choices with this continuing question always in the background.
>
> *Public Papers of the Presidents of the United States: Dwight D. Eisenhower.* January 1 to December 31, 1959 (Washington, D.C.: United States Government Printing Office, 1960), p. 570.

In the following year, John F. Kennedy, prior to becoming president on January 20, 1961, expressed his view of a truly democratic society on October 31, 1960, by underpinning his thoughts with a reference to Lincoln's triad. The fact that he mixed up the order of the three prepositions did not take anything away from his heartfelt explanation:

> I believe in an America with a government of men devoted solely to the public interest – men of ability and dedication, free from conflict or corruption or other commitment – a responsible government that is efficient and economical, with a balanced budget over the years of the cycle, reducing its debt in prosperous times – a government willing to entrust the people with the facts that they have – not businessman's government, with business in the saddle, not a labor government, not a farmer's government, not a government of one section of the country or another, but a government of, for, and by the people.
>
> Cited from David B. Frost (ed.), *John F. Kennedy in Quotations. A Topical Dictionary with Sources* (Jefferson, North Carolina: McFarland, 2013), p. 111.

Again and again one observes how sacrosanct Lincoln's words can become in serious sociopolitical matters. The Gettysburg Address is, of course, a national treasure, and the entire text or parts of it are often recited. In fact, on November 19, 1963, the *New York Times* republished it on the 100th anniversary of the short but pregnant speech (see "Lincoln's Gettysburg Address: Today Is Its 100th Anniversary," *The New York Times* (November 19, 1963), p. 35). And the last sentence, long proverbial in American parlance, once again reminded readers of this unique and memorable definition of democracy. A week and a half later, President John F. Kennedy was assassinated on November 22, 1963. The citizens of Hyannis Port, Massachusetts, where the Kennedy family has a home, passed the following resolution that paraphrased Lincoln's solemn address to honor the slain Kennedy: "We hereby highly resolve that John F. Kennedy shall not have died in vain, that each one of us, under God, shall do everything possible to eliminate any ideas of hatred, intolerance or revenge in our own hearts to the end that government of the people, by the people and for the people, shall not perish from the earth" (cited from Homer Bigart, "Mrs. Kennedy Spends Rainy Day in Seclusion," *The New York Times* (November 30, 1963), p. 13). During those sad times, this short statement, spoken by the people, was most appropriate to pay tribute to John F. Kennedy and to proclaim the survival of the American democracy.

About two months into his elected term as President of the United States, Lyndon B. Johnson, who had taken over the helm after Kennedy's assassination, issued a proclamation on "Loyalty Day" on March 11, 1965, starting with a quotation from the Declaration of Independence followed by Lincoln's well-worn phrase:

> "We hold these truths to be self-evident that all men are created equal, that they are endowed by their Creator with certain unalienable Rights, that among these are Life, Liberty and the pursuit of Happiness."
>
> With these words our forefathers proclaimed a revolutionary concept of human rights – a concept that permeates our Constitution and our democratic form of government. Less than a century later President Lincoln spoke of the United States as "this government of the people, by the people, and for the people."
>
> Our Nation's rise to its unequaled position of prosperity and power was no accident of fate – nor was it achieved without costly struggle. Rather, the United States flourished because her people were so dedicated to free government that they were willing to sacrifice their lives and fortunes, at home or abroad, to preserve our democratic institutions. The roll of our honored dead attests to the courage of our people.
>
> This loyalty of our people – their unswerving devotion to our Nation and its Constitution has rewarded us with a heritage of freedom never before achieved by any civilization. We must cherish that heritage and fulfill our sacred trust to enrich and preserve it for our children, and our children's children.
>
> In these times when misguided forces throughout the world publicly declare their intent to destroy our democratic way of life, we affirm again our eternal hostility to tyranny and oppression wherever it exists. Once more we proclaim our loyalty to the United States, our determination to preserve freedom, justice, equality, and human dignity in this land, and our resolution to assure these blessings for all who yearn to be free.
>
> https://www.presidency.uscb.edu/documents/proclamation-3643-loyaly-day-1965

Those words were proclaiming a special "Loyalty Day" with President Johnson surely having the war in Vietnam in mind that was causing upheavals here in the United States. While he did not go so far as to call for a loyalty oath among the population, he expected Americans to support the policies of the government.

Of course, President Richard Milhaus Nixon was also burdened with the war in Vietnam, taking the opportunity during his "State of the Union Address" of January 22, 1971, to repeat Johnson's call for the maintenance of the American democracy with the citizens being the very core. He does not merely cite Lincoln's proverbial triad but follows it up strategically with concise sentences that end with one of the three well-known prepositional phrases:

> Over the years we have added departments and created agencies at the federal level, each to serve a new constituency, to handle a particular task – and these have grown and multiplied in what has become a hopeless confusion of form and function.
>
> The time has come to match our structure to our purposes – to look with a fresh eye, to organize the government by conscious, comprehensive design to meet the new needs of a new era.
>
> One hundred years ago, Abraham Lincoln stood on a battlefield and spoke of a "government of the people, by the people, for the people." Too often since then, we have become a nation of the government, by the government, for the government.
>
> By enacting these reforms, we can renew that principle that Lincoln stated so simply and so well.
>
> By giving everyone's voice a chance to be heard, we will have a government that truly is of the people.
>
> By creating more centers of meaningful power, more places where decisions that really count can be made, by giving more people a chance to do something, we can have government that truly is by the people.
>
> And by setting up a completely modern, functional system of government at the national level, we in Washington will at last be able to provide government that is truly for the people.
>
> *Public Papers of the Presidents of the United States: Richard Milhaus Nixon.* 1971 (Washington, D.C.: United States Government Printing Office, 1922), pp. 56–57.

As Nixon was arguing against "big" government, he underpinned this vision by creating the anti-triad of America having "become a nation of the government, by the government, for the government." In formulating this ingenious parody, he probably recalled a statement that he had made earlier as a presidential candidate during remarks on the CBS Radio Network on June 27, 1968:

> When we look closely, we see that much of what is lacking in our society today is precisely what America was established to provide. Ours was conceived, in the eloquent simplicity of Lincoln's words, as a government of the people, by the people, and for the people. As we look back at this middle third of the century, we find that we have been getting more and more government for the people, but less and less government of the people and by the people.
>
> https://www.ucsb.edu/documents/remarks-the-cbs-radio-network-toward-expanded-democracy

Of course, not every use of Lincoln's phrase appears in political surroundings at the national level. There was also the 1964-poster at Calvin Coolidge High School proclaiming that "Government of the Students, by the Students, for the Students, shall not perish from Calvin Coolidge" (cited from Bel Kaufman, *Up the Down Staircase* (Englewood Cliffs, New Jersey: Prentice-Hall, 1964), p. 1390). And then came the corruption of the Nixon presidency with its Watergate scandal. Adlai E. Stevenson, Jr., Democratic Senator from Illinois, made effective use of the proverb in his Senate speech of October 2, 1972, by expanding it to show how President Richard Nixon negated its accepted truth: "The people are left to conclude what they will. And they will conclude that Mr. Nixon's Administration, because it will not permit an impartial investigation of the charges against it, has a great deal to hide. They are left to conclude that government of the people, by the people, for the people has given way, in Mr. Nixon's Washington, to the politics of wealth and stealth. And they are left to conclude that the era of the New Deal and the era of the Fair Deal have given way to Mr. Nixon's era: the Era of the Deal" (cited from *The New York Times* (October 3, 1972), p. 2). All of this led Theodore M. Hesburgh, president of the University of Notre Dame, to ask the following question: "Have we become so inured to unethical behavior on the part of those who govern us that we are beyond surprise or indignation whatever the crime? How did we come to such a sorry pass, we who pride ourselves on government of the people, by the people, for the people, with liberty and justice for all?" (cited from *The New York Times* (May 23, 1973),

p. 47). As will be remembered, Vice President Gerald Ford took over the reins after Nixon's disgraceful fall from the highest office of the land. The new president did his best to heal the political and moral wounds, and in his State of the Union Message of January 12, 1977, he began his remarks by reassuring the American people that the United States will carry on: "We can be confident, however, that 100 years from now a freely elected President will come before a freely elected Congress, chosen to renew our great republic's pledge to government of the people, by the people and for the people" (*Public Papers of the Presidents of the United States: Gerald Ford*. July 10, 1976 to January 20, 1977 (Washington, D.C.: United States Government Printing Office, 1979), p. 2916.). This was an effective way to start this speech as the American nation was beginning its third century with new hope for a more perfect people's government.

Jimmy Carter began his presidency with new confidence in the future hoping to make the government one that was there for the people. During his "State of the Union Address" of January 19, 1978, he addressed this matter by citing a truncated version only of Lincoln's triad. Since he mentioned the revered president's name as well, one can't help but wonder why he did not state the tripartite phrase in its entirety:

> During these past years, Americans have seen our Government grow far from us.
>
> For some citizens, the Government has almost become like a foreign country, so strange and distant that we've often had to deal with it through trained ambassadors who have sometimes become too powerful and too influential – lawyers, accountants, and lobbyists. This cannot go on.
>
> We must have what Abraham Lincoln wanted – a government for the people.
>
> We've made progress toward that kind of government. You've given me the authority I requested to reorganize the Federal bureaucracy. And I am using that authority.
>
> *Public Papers of the Presidents of the United States: Jimmy Carter*. January 1 to June 30, 1978 (Washington, D.C.: United States Government Printing Office, 1979), p. 94.

By the time of the national election of 1980, however, there was once again the worry that not enough people would take advantage of the great privilege and right of voting for their national government. The journalist Laurin Hall Healy commented on this malaise in an article in the *Christian Science Monitor* of November 3, 1980, effectively concluding it with Lincoln's phrase:

> American democracy cannot survive unless it has an informed, educated, and concerned citizenry actively involved in the political process. Apathy must be overcome. The idea must be eliminated that "what difference does it make who is elected?" – that "politicians are all crooked, and no matter which party wins the people always lose." [...] Tomorrow there will be more than 157 million Americans of voting age. If past experience holds true only 84 million of them will bother to go to the polls on election day. Will the other 73 million remain in the huge third party – the No-Vote Party? Or will an enhanced sense of these perilous times arouse the silent ones to stand up and be counted in defense of that unique experiment in government of the people, by the people, and for the people?
>
> Laurin Hall Healy, "Eight Weapons Against the No-Vote Party," *Christian Science Monitor* (November 3, 1980), p. 23.

This is all true, but voter apathy is at least to some degree understandable when one considers the modern ways of campaigns being influenced by lobbyists: "Those TV spots, that no politician can run for office without, have all but turned 'government of the people, by the people and for the people' into government of the lobbyists, by the lobbyists and for the lobbyists. And you can blame television for that" (*The New York Times* (April 4, 1999), p. SM19). What is needed, of course, is a broad educational process in politics. *The New York Times* certainly tries its best at it, giving people a chance to voice their opinions as well, as a self-advertisement of May 3, 1981, demonstrates. The headline reads: "Of the people, by the people, for the people." This is followed by a picture of Congress with two people reading the *Times*. Underneath is the slogan: "The Op-Ed Page. Every morning. The place to look for interesting ideas. *The New York Times*" (*The New York Times* (May 3, 1981), p. R11). And there was also the advertisement by WOR Radio of New York with the headline and caption containing the following message: "RADIO OF THE PEOPLE, BY THE PEOPLE, FOR THE PEOPLE. Beginning tomorrow and continuing through 1983, WOR Radio will bring you a contemporary essay on America. It will be a revelation to anyone who wants to understand the American Spirit. We'll explore the country from Boston Harbor to San Francisco Bay: We'll meet and talk with teachers, truck drivers, factory workers and mayors [...]"

(*The New York Times* (February 23, 1983), p. C23). And why not also high government officials, who hopefully are mindful that they represent a government of the people, by the people, for the people!

President Ronald Reagan was a strong proponent against the so-called "big government" as expressed in his inaugural address of January 20, 1981 by way of the quotable "Government is not the solution, it is the problem" statement. It certainly is a succinct summary of much of Reagan's political philosophy, i.e., his fight against excessive spending and regulation by the government at the expense of free interchange:

> In this present crisis, government is not the solution to our problem; government is the problem. From time to time we've been tempted to believe that society has become too complex to be managed by self-rule, that government by an elite group is superior to government for, by, and of the people. Well, if no one among us is capable of governing himself, then who among us has the capacity to govern someone else? All of us together, in and out of government, must bear the burden. The solutions we seek must be equitable, with no one group singled out to pay a higher price.
>
> *Public Papers of the Presidents of the United States: Ronald Reagan*. January 20 to December 31, 1981 (Washington, D.C.: United States Government Printing Office, 1982), p. 1.

And what a stroke of genius to add the shortest and best-known definition of democracy to it, with most Americans associating "Government of the people, by the people, and for the people" with Abraham Lincoln having said it at the end of his famous Gettysburg Address of November 19, 1863. Never mind that the order of the three prepositions is somewhat mixed up in the inaugural address. Reagan continued to cite the proverbial triad numerous times during his presidency, to wit just these four representative references:

> I believe this first 6 months of 1981 is going to mark the beginning of a new renaissance in America. Now we can face the future with confidence and courage, because we know we're united, and we know that we are a government of the people, by the people, and for the people. No one should doubt the difficulties we still face, but we have made a new beginning. We're back on the right road; we're making progress. And if we keep working together, we can reach that new era of prosperity that we all want. And as we do, we'll be

showing the world that our democratic system of government works because you, the people, make it work.

Washington, D.C.; July 29, 1981. *Public Papers of the Presidents of the United States: Ronald Reagan*. January 20 to December 31, 1981 (Washington, D.C.: United States Government Printing Office, 1982), p. 675.

We've made a new beginning. We've said goodbye to that philosophy of government – or that philosophy, I should say, of government knows best that was dragging America down. And we've restored the one driving idea that made America great – here the people rule; here in America we're a government of, by, and for the people, and not the other way around.

Macon, Georgia; October 15, 1984. *Public Papers of the Presidents of the United States: Ronald Reagan*. June 30 to December 31, 1984 (Washington, D.C.: United States Government Printing Office, 1987). p. 1537.

This year we most appropriately observe Immigrants Day on October 28, the 101st anniversary of the unveiling of the Statue of Liberty, the beloved statue Emma Lazarus called "Mother of Exiles," from whose "beacon-hand/Glows world-wide welcome." That welcome is America's welcome, which has ever beckoned millions upon millions of courageous souls to this land of freedom, justice, and opportunity.

Immigrants have always brought great gifts to their new home on these shores – the gifts of hardiness and heart, of intellect and hope. Two hundred years ago, immigrants were among the framers of a Constitution for these United States. They knew what they were about, for they began that charter of liberty and limited government with the words, "We the People" and created what a future President named Lincoln would call "government of the people, by the people, for the people."

Washington, D.C.; October 16, 1987. *Public Papers of the Presidents of the United States: Ronald Reagan*. July 4 to December 31, 1987 (Washington, D.C.: United States Government Printing Office, 1989), pp. 1189–1190.

And let me tell you, the thrill of standing in that place where so many great Presidents have stood and of continuing a tradition that stretches back to George Washington and signifies our determination that, as Lincoln said, a government of, by, and for the people shall not perish from the Earth – well that thrill never goes away.

Washington, D.C.; January 23, 1988. *Public Papers of the Presidents of the United States: Ronald Reagan*. January 1 to July 1, 1988 (Washington, D.C.: United States Government Printing Office, 1990), pp. 79–80.

But it must also be remembered that Ralph Nader criticized the Reagan administration on January 16, 1989, with this satirical comment: "This is a regime that came in on a philosophy of establishing a government of Exxon, by General Motors and for du Pont."

Of course, presidential candidates are also quite aware of the emotional power of Lincoln's democratic proverb that resonates so well in the minds of Americans. Democrat Walter Mondale, for example, made the following remarks on the political stomp against the reelection of Ronald Reagan in February of 1984: "Most Americans are never going to make a lot of money. They're going to live on modest incomes. But in America, we don't measure people by money. We measure people by what they really are. And when we talk about government of the people, by the people and for the people, that's what we mean. But what we've got today is a government of the rich, by the rich, and for the rich" (Walter F. Mondale, "3 Things That We Must Do Together," *The New York Times* (February 22, 1984), p. A18). He liked his substitution of "rich" for "people" so much that he repeated this variant in his address accepting the Democratic Party nomination for President on July 19, 1984: "Four years ago, many of you voted for Mr. Reagan because he promised that you'd be better off. And today, the rich are better off. But working Americans are worse off, and the middle class is standing on a trap door. Lincoln once said that ours is to be a government of the people, by the people, and for the people. But what we have today is a government of the rich, by the rich, and for the rich and we're going to make a change in November" (cited from the "Transcript of Mondale Address Accepting Party Nomination," *The New York Times* (July 20, 1984), p. A2). Mondale was not elected, voter turn-out was once again not impressive, and when three years later the country celebrated two hundred years of the Constitution, the question was raised: "Is this still 'government of the people, by the people, and for the people'? Are 'We the people' turned off politics?" (Charlotte Saikowski, "Two Hundred Years of the Constitution – Can America Govern Itself?" *Christian Science Monitor* (February 13, 1987), p. 20. Such are the perils of a democracy, but in typical American fashion of looking forward, hope springs eternal that citizens will make it their responsibility that their government is based on the free choices of the people themselves.

Hand-picked by Ronald Reagan as his successor, President George Bush continued the policy of shrinking the role that the federal government should play, taking the opportunity of a proclamation of March 19, 1991 on "National County Government Week" to expound on this theme:

> National County Government Week is a fitting time to reaffirm the continued importance of a strong partnership between City, County, State, and Federal Government – particularly in areas such as education, transportation, and the fight against drug abuse. In recent years, more and more Americans have realized what many have known all along: that the answer to many of the problems before us can be found, not in bigger Federal Government, but in effective local leadership and cooperation between citizens and public officials at all levels. Indeed, we know that government closest to the people is truly government "of the people, by the people, and for the people." This is the essence of federalism and democracy, and it is the key to meeting many of the challenges and opportunities before our country.
>
> https://www.presidency.ucsb.edu/documents/proclamation-6261-national-county-government-week-1991

It might also be remembered that the popular hit "Banned in the USA" (1990) by 2Live Crew was somewhat directed against the restriction of free speech early during George Bush's presidency. It contained the lines:

> Freedom of speech will never die
> For us to have, our ancestors died
> Don't keep thinking that we will quit
> We'll always stand and never sit
> [...]
>
> The First Amendment gave us freedom of speech
> So what you sayin', it didn't include me?
> I like to party and have a good time
> There's nothin' but pleasure written in our rhymes
> I know you don't think we'll ever quit
> We've got some people on our side who won't take your lip
> We're gonna do all the things we wanna do
> [...]
> Banned in the U-S-A, I was
> [...]
>
> The United States of America
> Government of the people
> The United States of America
> For the people

> The United States of America
> By the people
> https://www.google.com/search?q=2+live+crew+banned+in+the+usa+lyrics&rlz

It must not be forgotten that popular culture in the form of songs, posters, cartoons, etc. does its part in integrating traditional quotations or proverbs into the concerns of the modern age. But speaking of freedom of speech also brings to mind the issue of freedom of information from the national archives, most effectively expressed in the following paragraph and the title of the article from which it is cited:

> As public trusts, the nation's archives must continue to be open and accessible to all without cost. More than a mere statement of principle, this is a necessary element of the peer-production system. The results: archives whose holdings are much easier to discover, access, and use. And the bonus is a community of highly intelligent men and women who will come to understand and appreciate archives. The archives of the people (as they have always been, but only in the abstract) thus become the archives by the people (who contribute and add value) and for the people (who now can actually use them). Archives thus become a part not only of the information economy, but of the knowledge and creative economy. [...] Archival institutions must reinvent themselves, in collaboration with other archives and with other types of organizations, to systematically invite and encourage commons-based peer-production. The archives of, by, and for the people demand no less.
>
> Max J. Evans, "Archives of the People, by the People, for the People," *American Archivist*, 70 (2007), pp. 387–400.

But to return to the presidents, Bill Clinton in his "Message on the Observance of Presidents' Day" of February 17, 1996, paid homage to two great former presidents, somewhat predictably to Washington and Lincoln. While George Bush had included the "people"-triad without reference to Lincoln, Clinton added the name of the admired president to it as he recalled, albeit indirectly, his struggle during the Civil War:

> America has been blessed with many great and good leaders over the past two centuries. The Presidents we honor with special pride on this day – Goerge Washington and Abraham Lincoln – accepted the burdens of their office at moments of great national challenge and set a shining example for those who were to follow.

> As the first President of the United States, Washington played a vital part in defining the role of the Presidency in America's government and national life. With courage and vision, he ensured the steady course of American democracy and, in relinquishing his office at the appointed time, established the peaceful transition of power that has become the envy of other nations around the world.
>
> Abraham Lincoln preserved the Union that Washington helped to create. He guided America through four years of painful and bloody conflict, and at the end of his Presidency, we were still one nation under God, and government "of the people, by the people, and for the people" had not perished from our land.
>
> But Presidents alone cannot assure America's success or preserve our freedom for future generations. It falls to each and every citizen to take part in the great experiment of American democracy.
>
> *Public Papers of the Presidents of the United States: William J. Clinton*. January 1 to June 30, 1996. (Washington, D.C.: United States Government Printing Office, 1997), p. 296.

This short statement, somewhat of a concise history lesson, contains much expected proverbial wisdom, but there is more to it. Clinton does not only cite the democratic proverb but also mentions that George Washington exemplifies the orderly transfer of presidential power in the United States – a lesson that needs to be remembered as this very concept is being challenged in the present time. In retrospect these comments take on a clairvoyant aspect in regard to the January 6, 2021, takeover of the Capitol as President Donald Trump and his followers were contesting the result of the national election that had named Joe Biden to be the next president. Here then is a powerful statement by Bill Clinton on the day of the assault on the Capitol:

> Today we faced an unprecedented assault on our Capitol, our Constitution, and our country.
>
> The assault was fueled by more than four years of poison politics spreading deliberate misinformation, sowing distrust in our system, and pitting Americans against one another. The match was lit by Donald Trump and his most ardent enablers, including many in Congress, to overturn the results of an election he lost.
>
> The election was free, the count was fair, the result is final. We must complete the peaceful transfer of power our Constitution mandates.

> I have always believed that America is made up of good, decent people. I still do. If that's who we really are, we must reject today's violence, turn the page, and move forward together – honoring our Constitution, remaining committed to a government of the people, by the people, and for the people.
>
> https://www.clintonfoundation.org/press-and-news/general/statement-president-clinton-assualt-capitol/

If anybody ever were to maintain that Lincoln's democratic proverb has become clichéd, let them read this spontaneous reaction and many others presented in this study for that matter.

Earlier on October 17, 1996, during a reelection campaign stop on October 17, 1996, Bill Clinton committed an odd gaffe that gave his opponent Robert Dole the opportunity to ridicule the president. Clinton must have left his manuscript or spoke spontaneously, causing him to get the facts about Lincoln's proverbial triad mixed up:

> Our friends on the other side [the Republicans], they complain about government all the time. They set it up as the enemy, it's government versus the people.
>
> The last time I checked, the Constitution said, of the people, by the people and for the people.
>
> That's what the Declaration of Independence says. That's why, even though we have abolished more regulations, ended more programs, and reduced the size of the Government more than our predecessors did, we have also done more to create opportunity, to reinforce responsibility, and to bring the American people into a community together instead of always dividing us. I am tired of that. I want us to go forward, and I think you do, too.
>
> *Public Papers of the Presidents of the United States: William J. Clinton*. July 1 to December 31, 1996 (Washington, D.C.: United States Government Printing Office, 1998), p. 1860.

Such misstatements are bound to happen during political campaigns and most certainly are not signs of a lack of cultural literacy. In any case, when President Clinton employed the democratic proverb once again on March 26, 1998, at Cape Town, South Africa, he did much better in expressing the sincere hope that more countries in the world might create governments based on the triad:

> As I look out at all of you I see our common promise. Two centuries ago, the courage and imagination that created the United States and the principle[s] that are enshrined in our Constitution inspired men and women without a voice across the world to believe that one day they, too, could have a government of the people, by the people, and for the people. Now, the courage and imagination that created the new South Africa and the principles that guide your Constitution inspire all of us to be animated by the belief that one day humanity all the world over can at last be released from the bonds of hatred and bigotry.
>
> *Public Papers of the Presidents of the United States: William J. Clinton*. January 1 to June 30, 1998 (Washington, D.C.: United States Government Printing Office, 1999), p. 442.

And there is also an amazing story that his wife, Hillary Rodham Clinton, recalls in her book *An Invitation to the White House: At Home with History* (New York: Simon & Schuster, 2000: 61). The Clintons had welcomed leaders from China to the White House in an attempt to improve relations between the two countries: "I will never forget Premier Zhu Ronji of China recalling in his toast that he had memorized the Gettysburg Address as a schoolboy. He recited a section from memory, including the phrase 'of the people, by the people, for the people' – a hope we hold for the Chinese people." It is good to know that Lincoln's phrase continues to conquer the world as a symbol of democratic government!

The Democratic Proverb in the Twenty-First Century

But speaking of politics, Lincoln's proverb was even utilized during the national crisis of September 11, 2001, when the American democracy was shaken by dreadful terrorist attacks. The reaction to this tragedy took many forms, but here is the comment by Kathryn L. van Heyningen from Palm Harbor, Florida, who as a citizen had this to say in the *St. Petersburg Times*: "Though the World Trade Center was demolished, the Pentagon damaged, we must remember that this country is more than glass, steel and concrete. The terrorists struck at symbols of our nation, but it is the people who make a country great. We cannot and will not live in fear. We will not surrender, and as Lincoln said: 'The government of the people, by the people and for the people shall not perish from this earth'" (Kathryn L. van Heyningen, "Our Steely Determination," *St. Petersburg Times* (September 16, 2001), p. 6D). This short paragraph was indeed a rhetorically and emotionally appropriate reaction to this terrible tragedy. For several days and even weeks similar heartfelt and patriotic comments appeared in print or were expressed orally in the mass media. The same was true, of course, around the days of the first anniversary of the attack on America. And yet, everyday life has once again engulfed the country, and there is no lack of mundane phrases and slogans to mark a modern existence devoid of the depth of the wisdom expressed by Abraham Lincoln and some of the other great presidents before and after him. The colorful promotional book by Adam Kipple, Andrew Kipple, and Luke Wherry with the title *People of Walmart: Of the People, by the People, for the People* (Naperville, Illinois: Sourcebook, 2012) might serve as an example of a superficial use of the phrase. In any case, today's political rhetoric does also not seem to measure up any longer to the lofty heights of the remarks by some of these national leaders. The journalist Tim Cuprisin made this point on January 2, 2002, in his satirical article "'Dead Body' Phrase May Mark Bush's Political Life" by contrasting Lincoln's proverb and two of Franklin D. Roosevelt's memorable phrases with the inane utterances of recent presidents:

> It's still too early to tell, but we just may have witnessed one of those landmark presidential sound bites over the weekend. It wasn't one of the stately phrases that presidents once uttered, like Abraham Lincoln's "government of the people, by the people and for the people" or Franklin D. Roosevelt's "we have nothing to fear but fear itself," or "a date which will live in infamy." We're talking about the TV age, when a short burst of simple, almost trivial, words caught on videotape, like Richard Nixon's "I'm not a crook," can characterize an entire presidency. For George Bush the elder, it was, of course, "read my lips, no new taxes." He, of course, went on to ignore those lips. And no one can dispute that Bill Clinton's "I did not have sexual relations with that woman" is likely the most famous lie ever uttered on camera from behind a straight face. For George W. Bush, there's a good chance that Saturday's "not over my dead body will they raise your taxes" will enter that pantheon of presidential sound bites, although he meant what he said. He's just as sincere as his dad was back in 1988.
>
> Tim Cuprisin, "'Dead Body' Phrase May Mark Bush's Political Life," *Milwaukee Journal Sentinel* (January 8, 2002), p. 6B.

One thing is for certain, however, Lincoln's proverbial triad appears to be ready-made for presidential proclamations, as can be observed from President George W. Bush's comments on "Citizenship Day and Constitution Week" on September 16, 2003:

> Our Constitution and our country have grown stronger over the last 216 years – through wars, searing internal conflicts, and great social, economic, and technological change. In the last 2 years, America has again been tested, this time by terrorist attacks designed to strike our people, our institutions, and our constitutional government. In the wake of those attacks, we have renewed and strengthened our commitment to a more perfect Union and common defense, to justice and domestic tranquility, to the general welfare and the blessings of liberty.
>
> On Citizenship Day and during Constitution Week, we remember those who fought and those who died to preserve, protect, and defend the Constitution. We recall and reiterate the vow of President Abraham Lincoln that these "dead shall not have died in vain – that this Nation, under God, shall have a new birth of freedom – and that government of the people, by the people, for the people, shall not perish from the earth."
>
> https://www.presidency.ucsb.edu/documents/proclamation-7705-citizenship-day-and-constitution-week-2003

Barack Obama, on his way to his presidential inauguration, repeated the following words on January 17, 2009, at Philadelphia and at Baltimore that are as celebratory as those of President Bush in their recollection of historical phraseology:

> And yet, they [early patriots] were willing to put all they were and all they had on the line – their lives, their fortunes and their sacred honor – for a set of ideals that continue to light the world. That we are equal. That our rights to life, liberty and the pursuit of happiness come not from our laws, but from our maker. And that government of, by and for the people can endure. It was these ideals that led us to declare independence and craft our constitution, producing documents that were imperfect but had within them, like our nation itself, the capacity to be made more perfect.
>
> https://www.presidency.ucsb.edu/documents/address-during-the-inaugural-whistle-stop-tour-baltimore

The enthusiastic crowd would surely have recognized Obama's references to the beginning of the Declaration of Independence as well as Lincoln's democratic proverb. However, they might well have missed the allusion to the little-known final sentence of Jefferson's text: "And for the support of this Declaration, with a firm Reliance on the Protection of divine Providence, we mutually pledge to each other our Lives, our Fortunes, and our sacred Honor."

Early in his presidency, Barack Obama delivered one of his greatest speeches on June 4, 2009 at Cairo, Egypt. He had expressed his positive forward-looking worldview in his book *The Audacity of Hope. Thoughts on Reclaiming the American Dream* (New York: Crown Publishers, 2006), and he was eager to spread the "hopeful gospel" far beyond the borders of the United States. And there he was in front of five thousand students at Cairo University, reaching out to the Muslim world as no modern American president had done before. It was a phenomenal speech, interrupted repeatedly by cheers of approval by the students. President Obama argued forcefully against negative stereotypes of Islam, but he was quick to point out that eradicating the world of stereotypes must involve people everywhere, who, after all, were all created equal, as Obama never ceased to point out proverbially:

> Just as Muslims do not fit a crude stereotype, America is not the crude stereotype of a self-interested empire. The United States has been one of the greatest sources of progress that the world has ever known. We were born out of revolution against an empire. We were founded upon the ideal that all are created equal, and we have shed blood and struggled for centuries to give meaning to those words – within our borders, and around the world. We are shaped by every culture, drawn from every end of the earth, and dedicated to a simple concept: E pluribus unum – "Out of many, one".
>
> *Public Papers of the Presidents of the United States: Barack Obama*. January 20 to June 30, 2009 (Washington, D.C.: United States Government Printing Office, 2010), p. 765.

The old classical proverb "E pluribus unum" which is part of the American seal embodies Obama's vision of a world in which people emphasize their similarities rather than stress their differences. And this view includes a democratic form of government, of course, as Obama stresses by citing part of the proverbial triad of a "government of the people, by the people, for the people":

> There are some who advocate for democracy only when they're out of power; once in power, they are ruthless in suppressing the rights of others. So no matter where it takes hold, government of the people and by the people sets a single standard for all who would hold power: You must maintain your power through consent, not coercion; you must respect the rights of minorities, and participate with a spirit of tolerance and compromise; you must place the interests of your people and the legitimate workings of the political process above your party. Without these ingredients, elections alone do not make a true democracy.
>
> *Public Papers of the Presidents of the United States: Barack Obama*. January 20 to June 30, 2009 (Washington, D.C.: United States Government Printing Office, 2010), pp. 765–766.

It is not clear why Obama does not cite the third element "for the people" of the proverbial definition, but what he does say surely refers to the fact that the government is there for the people whom it serves! And then, very close to the end of this moving and inspiring speech to thousands of Arabic students, he asked them "to reimagine the world, to remake this world." Little wonder that there were repeated applause and calls of the type "Barack Obama, we love you!" during the speech. The climax of the speech was reached when the President called for a new world of brother- and sisterhood informed by empathy and mutual respect, with the center of his powerful statement being occupied by the proverbial golden rule:

> All of us share this world for but a brief moment in time. The question is whether we spend that time focused on what pushes us apart, or whether we commit ourselves to an effort – a sustained effort – to find common ground, to focus on the future we seek for our children, and to respect the dignity of all human beings.
>
> It's easier to start wars than to end them. It's easier to blame others than to look inward. It's easier to see what is different about someone than to find the things we share. But we should choose the right path, not just the easy path. There's one rule that lies at the heart of every religion – that we do unto others as we would have them do unto us. This truth transcends nations and peoples – a belief that isn't new; that isn't black or white or brown; that isn't Christian or Muslim or Jew. It's a belief that pulsed in the cradle of civilization, and that still beats in the hearts of billions around the world. It's a faith in other people, and it's what brought me here today.

> *Public Papers of the Presidents of the United States: Barack Obama*. January 20 to June 30, 2009 (Washington, D.C.: United States Government Printing Office, 2010), p. 768.

That is rational and emotional rhetoric, coming both from the mind and the heart, as it calls for a new world order based on ethical values that bind humankind together in the spirit of the humane golden rule.

It will perhaps come as no surprise that Bernie Sanders, the democratic socialist Senator from Vermont, also draws on the proverbial definition of democracy, i.e., "Government of the people, by the people, for the people." In his book *Our Revolution* (2016) Sanders recalls a visit to Gettysburg in February of 2015 where he was deeply moved by the monuments commemorating this major battle of the Civil War in Pennsylvania. He recalls Lincoln's famous speech with the proverbial triad and then observes that with the Supreme Court having decided to put no limits on campaign donations by corporations, the very basis of American democracy is in jeopardy:

> We also visited the site where Lincoln gave his famous address in 1863. As every schoolchild knows, in his speech Lincoln stated "that we here highly resolve that these dead shall not have died in vain ... that this nation, under God, shall have a new birth of freedom ... and that government of the people, by the people, for the people, shall not perish from the earth." As we left Gettysburg, it struck me forcefully that what Lincoln had said in 1863 was as relevant today as it was back then. Especially with the Supreme Court's disastrous 2010 Citizens United decision that opened the floodgates to virtually unlimited corporate spending in campaigns and allowed big money to buy elections, we were still fighting for a government "of the people, by the people, for the people." As a result of that trip to Gettysburg, I often referenced Lincoln, and what he said there on that day in 1863, in my speeches.
>
> Bernie Sanders, *Our Revolution. A Future to Believe in* (New York: St. Martin's Press, 2016). p. 81.

Indeed, the proverbial triad became somewhat of a leitmotif for Sanders to this day, as he crisscrosses the nation in his crusade to overcome the unfortunate truth of the nineteenth-century proverb "The rich get richer, and the poor get poorer." Sanders returns twice to Lincoln's democratic definition in his book. With honesty and humility he states that America has tried to make its government more inclusive, but clearly the ideal state has by no means been reached:

> We also know, however, that the Constitution they drafted, while revolutionary in its day, reflected the values and mores of the 1790s: slavery and racism, rigid class lines, and a deeply rooted sexism. We know that since then, amidst bloodshed, struggle, and turmoil, the American people have sought to expand democracy and make it more inclusive. To quote Lincoln at Gettysburg, our goal has been to create "a government of the people, by the people and for the people." (pp. 186–187)
>
> Bernie Sanders, *Our Revolution. A Future to Believe in* (New York: St. Martin's Press, 2016), pp. 186–187.

His use of "the American people" rather than Americans in many ways pays homage to the longer phrase "of, by, and for the people" because it grounds decisions in the popular consent of the citizens. And then, barely 30 pages later, he quotes the pertinent passage from Lincoln's address once again, but this time he expresses his thoughts in an even more drastic and alarming fashion by citing the triad a total of two times. It all amounts to a proverbial warning that America's democratic government is in danger if campaign finance reforms will not be forthcoming to control the influence of big business and wealthy people.

> On November 19, 1863, standing on the bloodstained battlefield of Gettysburg, Pennsylvania, Abraham Lincoln delivered one of the best-remembered speeches in American history. At the conclusion of his Gettysburg Address, Lincoln stated "that we here highly resolve that these dead shall not have died in vain … that this nation, under God, shall have a new birth of freedom … and that government of the people, by the people, for the people, shall not perish from the earth." In the year 2016, with a political campaign finance system that is corrupt and increasingly controlled by billionaires and special interests, I fear very much that, in fact, "government of the people, by the people, for the people" will perish in the United States of America. […] The need for real campaign finance reform is not a progressive issue. It is not a conservative issue. It is an American issue. It is an issue that should concern all Americans – regardless of their political point of view – who wish to preserve the essence of the longest standing democracy in the world, a government that is supposed to represent all of the people and not just a handful of powerful special interests.
>
> Bernie Sanders, *Our Revolution. A Future to Believe in* (New York: St. Martin's Press, 2016), pp. 203–204.

Among the manipulating corporations are the giant banks that in Sanders's opinion have way too much power and influence not only on elections but on the entire American economy and beyond. In fact, it has been argued that some banks and financial institutions are so big that if they were to fail, the entire economy would collapse if the government were not to step in and bail them out. In other words, such financial powerhouses must not be allowed to fail. All of this brings to mind the major financial crisis of 2008 that led to calls for splitting such large conglomerates up. It was at this time that the slogan "If it is too big to fail, it is too big (to exist)" appeared on the horizon that somewhat indirectly calls for their downsizing. But here is one more very recent pertinent quotation from Bernie Sanders in which he juxtaposes Lincoln's famous words with his fight against the "billionaire class":

> As I was listening to [Donald] Trump's terrible speech [his inaugural address on January 20, 2025], I was remembering my American history. In 1863, a few days after the Battle of Gettysburg, where thousands of soldiers died fighting to end the abomination of slavery, Abraham Lincoln told the American people that "these dead shall not have died in vain, that this nation, under God, shall have a new birth of freedom, and that government of the people, by the people, for the people, shall not perish from the earth."
>
> Well. At Trump's inauguration I was witnessing, up in front, a very different vision of government. It was a government of the billionaire class, by the billionaire class, for the billionaire class. Not a pleasant sight.
>
> Bernie Sanders, *Fight Oligarchy* (New York: Crown, 2025), pp. 19–20.

As expected by now, President Joe Biden quite appropriately also called on Abraham Lincoln's proverbial wisdom in his speech during the opening session of the virtually held "The Summit for Democracy" on December 9, 2021, at Washington, D.C. With democracy being the theme, it was predictable that the president would cite the democratic proverb:

> Here in the United States, we know as well as anyone that renewing our democracy and strengthening our democratic institutions requires constant effort.
>
> American democracy is an ongoing struggle to live up to our highest ideals and to heal our divisions; to recommit ourselves to the founding idea of our nation captured in our Declaration of Independence.

> We say: "We hold these truths to be self-evident" that all women and men are created equal, endowed by their Creator with certain unalienable rights, among them life, liberty, and the pursuit of happiness.
>
> Democracy doesn't happen by accident. We have to renew it with each generation.
>
> […]
>
> Democracy – government of the people, by the people, for the people – can at times be fragile, but it also is inherently resilient. It's capable of self-correction and it's capable of self-improvement.
>
> https://bidenwhitehouse.archices.gov/briefing-room/speeches-remarks/2021/12/09/remarks-by-president-biden-at-the-summit-for-democracy-opening

In addition to his own declaration that "Democracy doesn't happen by accident," President Biden might well have enjoyed fellow-democrat Franklin D. Roosevelt's sententious remark "Democracy is not s static thing. It is an everlasting march" of October 1, 1935 (*The Public Papers and Addresses of Franklin D. Roosevelt, 1935* (New York: Random House, 1938), vol. 4, p. 405). Instead Biden states in his summit remarks that his friend "Congressman John Lewis was a great champion of American democracy and for civil rights around the world, learning from and gaining from other great leaders like Gandhi and Mandela. With his final words, as he was dying, to our nation last year, he reminded our country, quote, 'Democracy is not a state, it is an act'." But as a third modern definition of a democratic government let me add "Democracy is a process, not an end point" that President Ronald Reagan pronounced in a speech of February 24, 1988 (*Public Papers of the Presidents of the United States: Ronald Reagan*, 1 January to 3 July 1988 (Washington, D.C.: U.S. Government Printing Office, 1990), p. 266). These three definition attempts certainly deserve to be registered in new editions of quotation dictionaries as they express the ever-evolving nature of democracies.

Finally, then, there is also President Domald Trump's very recent "Presidential Message on the Anniversary of the Gettysburg Address" of November 19, 2025. He found the right words to memorialize Abraham Lincoln's unforgettable words, concluding his remarks with the perfect definition of democracy:

> President Lincoln's message still reaches across time to remind us of our proud history, our common bond, and our duties as Americans. He called upon the people of this country in every age to stand as one Nation, preserve our liberty, and always defend our God-given right to self-government. As we prepare to celebrate 250 glorious years of American independence, we renew our commitment to those timeless principles and continue our work to ensure that our great Nation remains worthy of the ultimate sacrifices that built and preserved it. We will always remember our fallen heroes, cherish our freedom, honor our heritage, and forever uphold that a government of the people, by the people, and for the people, shall not perish from the earth.
>
> https://www.whitehouse.gov/briefings-statements/2025/11/america-250-presidential-message-on-the-anniversary-of-the-gettysburg-address/

In conclusion of this fascinating history of the democratic proverb "Government of the people, by the people, for the people," it might be appropriate that in these different and difficult times, when every word is recorded and together with pictures is broadcast instantly around the world, it behooves modern presidents to pay close attention to their rhetoric once again as their predecessors most assuredly practiced it. The words and phrases of spontaneous utterances as well as of formal addresses or speeches need to be chosen with considerable care, and a good dose of pride in the English language ought to be added to it. With such proper respect for the power of words, modern presidents as well can formulate statements that will be entered into the annals of American political and social history. In the meantime, Americans have Abraham Lincoln's proverb "Government of the people, by the people, for the people" to guide them in their attempt to make democracy work. It certainly is a piece of wisdom that might lead humankind with the assistance of the United Nations to a free and democratic world.

Bibliography

Aron, Paul. 2008. *We Hold These Truths … And Other Words that Made America*. Lanham, Maryland: Bowman & Littlefield.

Bartlett, John. 2012. *Bartlett's Familiar Quotations*, ed. Geoffrey O'Brien. 18th ed. New York: Little, Brown and Company.

Beasley, Vanessa B. *You the People. American National Identity in Presidential Rhetoric*. College Station, Texas: Texas A&M University Press.

Burrell, Brian. 1997. *The Words we Live By. The Creeds, Mottoes, and Pledges that Have Shaped America*. New York: The Free Press.

Campbell, Karlyn Kohrs, and Kathleen Hall Jamieson, 2008. *Presidents Creating the Presidency. Deed Done in Words*. Chicago: University of Chicago Press.

Fields, Wayne. 1996. *Union of Words. A History of Presidential Eloquence*, New York: Free Press.

Frost, Elizabeth. 1988. *The Bully Pulpit. Quotations from American Presidents*. New York: Facts on File.

Jay, Antony. 1996. *The Oxford Dictionary of Political Quotations*. Oxford: Oxford University Press.

Mieder, Wolfgang. 2000. *The Proverbial Abraham Lincoln. An Index to Proverbs in the Works of Abraham Lincoln*. New York: Peter Lang.

Mieder, Wolfgang. 2005. *Proverbs Are the Best Policy. Folk Wisdom and American Politics*. Logan, Utah: Utah State University Press.

Mieder, Wolfgang. 2012. *Proverbs Are Never Out of Season. Popular Wisdom in the Modern Ages*. New York: Peter Lang.

Mieder, Wolfgang. 2014. *Behold the Proverbs of a People. Proverbial Wisdom in Culture, Literature, and Politics*. Jackson, Mississippi: University Press of Mississippi.

Mieder, Wolfgang. 2019. *"Right Makes Might". Proverbs and the American Worldview*. Bloomington, India: Indiana University Press.

Mieder, Wolfgang. 2021. *Dictionary of Authentic American Proverbs*. New York: Berghahn Books.

Mieder, Wolfgang. 2025. *Worth a Thousand Words. Cultural, Literary, and Political Proverb Studies*. Jackson, Mississippi: University Press of Mississippi.

Obama, Barack. 2006. *The Audacity of Hope. Thoughts on Reclaiming the American Dream*. New York: Crown Publishers.

Sanders, Bernie. 2016. *Our Revolution. A Future to Believe in*. New York: St. Martin's Press.

Shapiro, Fred R. 2021. *The New Yale Book of Quotations*. New Haven, Connecticut: Yale University Press.

Tierney, John. 2016. *Conceived in Liberty. The American Worldview in Theory and Practice*. New Brunswick, New Jersey: Transaction Publishers.

Webber, Christopher L. 2014. *Give Me Liberty. Speakers and Speeches that Have Shaped America*. New York: Pegasus Books.

Wills, Garry. 1992. *Lincoln at Gettysburg: The Words that Remade America*. New York: Touchstone.

VECTORS

DEFINITION

Vectors are not like typical academic monographs. They are aimed at a more general audience, which might include undergraduate students, academics working in other fields, practitioners, policymakers, and the public. They provide a platform for established academic authors to reach a larger audience than usual, or to speak to new audiences; to deliver bold new arguments; to write unencumbered by the usual obligations for referencing; and to be exciting, provocative and even polemical.

ALREADY PUBLISHED:

Massimo Arcangeli, *Genderless Grammar.*
Alberto Lucarelli, *Tradition & Revolution.*
Eugenio Borgna, *Hope and Despair.*
Eugenio Borgna, *Wounded Nostalgia.*
Eugenio Borgna, *The Madness That is Also in Us.*
Wolfgang Mieder, *Proverbial Democracy: Government of the People, by the People, for the People.*

COMING SOON:

Simone Gozzano, *Consciousness.*

www.ingramcontent.com/pod-product-compliance
Ingram Content Group UK Ltd.
Pitfield, Milton Keynes, MK11 3LW, UK
UKHW021959190726
13853UKWH00004B/1626

9 783034 365673